unholiness

OVERCOMING THE FORCES THAT ATTACK YOUR SOUL

Christopher T. Bounds and Jim "Umfundisi" Lo

wesleyan
PUBLISHING HOUSE
wphstore.com

Copyright © 2015 by Christopher Bounds and Jim Lo
Published by Wesleyan Publishing House
Indianapolis, Indiana 46250
Printed in the United States of America
ISBN 978-0-89827-703-6
ISBN (e-book): 978-0-89827-704-3

Library of Congress Cataloging-in-Publication Data

Bounds, Christopher T.
 Unholiness : overcoming the forces that attack your soul / Christopher Bounds
and Jim Lo.
    pages cm
  ISBN 978-0-89827-703-6 (pbk.)
  1. Sin--Christianity. 2. Spiritual warfare. I. Title.
  BT715.B699 2015
  235'.4--dc23
                            2015017221

To the Norfork United Methodist Church,
where I (Chris) began to understand the beauty
and power of Christ's sanctifying grace.

To Rev. and Mrs. Andrew Gerleman
who modeled holiness for me (Jim)
when I was a young believer.

contents

Free shepherding resources are available at
www.wphresources.com/unholiness.

introduction
WHY FORGIVENESS IS NOT ENOUGH

She will give birth to a son, and you are to give him the
name Jesus, because he will save his people from their sins.

—Matthew 1:21

The one who does what is sinful is of the devil, because the devil
has been sinning from the beginning. The reason the Son
of God appeared was to destroy the devil's work.

—1 John 3:8

Sin is humanity's great enemy. If God loves us, he must save us
from this formidable foe. Therefore, when the angel Gabriel appeared
to Joseph to explain Mary's miraculous pregnancy, he told Joseph
to name the baby Jesus, because he would "save his people from their
sins" (Matt. 1:21). The apostle John reiterated Gabriel's declaration:
the Son of God came to "destroy the devil's work" (1 John 3:8), sin
and all its fruits. This was the purpose of the incarnation.

the problem of sin

The Scriptures use a number of images to describe the problem of sin. Perhaps the most well-known is the legal description (Rom. 4:15). Sin is the violation of God's law. God made clear what he expects of us and we disobey him.

In the Old Testament, God drew a clear line in the sand and warned our first parents of the penalty if they crossed it. He told Adam and Eve they could eat from any tree in the garden of Eden, but they must not eat from the Tree of Knowledge of Good and Evil or they would die (Gen. 2:17). The apostle Paul taught that God gave the Gentiles a clear internal code of conscience and the Jews a written law to follow, but both groups were guilty of deliberate disobedience and stood under divine condemnation with the sentence of death (Rom. 2:12–23; 3:23). Each of us has received some measure of light regarding what God requires of us, yet we have not always walked according to it. Our disobedience leaves us under God's condemnation. We stand guilty in God's court of law under the threat of death.

A second image is a social one (Jer. 11:10). Sin is the breaking of relationship. The creation account in Genesis pictures humanity as communal. Adam and Eve walked in intimacy with God, loved one another, and exercised caring stewardship of the created order. Jesus summarized the Old Testament's teaching on the chief end of humanity as a call to love God with all one's heart, soul, and mind and to love one's neighbor as oneself (Matt. 22:37–40).

Sin's problem is more than a broken law; it is the severing of relationship. It harms our relationship with God and also human social bonds. Therefore, the consequences of sin are described not only in terms of guilt, but also in terms of alienation, hostility, and divorce.

Through our sinful thoughts, words, and deeds, we have undermined the very relationships by which we gain ultimate meaning in life. We are estranged from God, each other, and the created order.

A final image of sin is taken from the Jewish temple and ceremonial law (Lev. 10:10). Sin is defilement or uncleanness. All instruments used in worship in the tabernacle were required to be "clean," set apart wholly for the purposes of God. They could not be desecrated, intentionally or unintentionally, physically, morally, or spiritually. Any type of contamination would render them unfit for use before a God of absolute holiness. The children of Israel were called to be a "holy nation," set apart from the sinfulness of the world for the purposes of God (Lev. 11:44–45). This call extends to the church in the New Testament (1 Pet. 1:15–16). The problem of sin, therefore, goes beyond the issues of guilt and alienation; it strikes at the very essence of humanity. Sin is a defilement that pollutes us and makes us unholy. Humanity was created in the image of God to be holy as God is holy. Sin is a soiling of human nature and the divine image in humanity. It makes humanity unsuitable for God.

Compounding these problems of sin is the power it exerts in human life. The Scriptures describe human beings as slaves to sin. While it might appear we have some degree of control over sin in our lives, in the end we are slaves to it. So much so, the apostle Paul wrote that even when we know what we are called to do, and even when we want to walk in obedience to God, too often we lack the power to follow through with our good intentions (Rom. 7:14–25). If we search our hearts, we find a bent or propensity toward rebellion, disobedience, and selfishness ruling our lives. A godly life of virtue, love of God, and love of neighbor do not come easily to us. Something inside us balks at what God requires of us. We resist what we know to be of God's will. Our will rises up and declares, "I won't." Or, if we have some desire to obey, it cries out, "I can't." We are not able to comply inwardly or outwardly with God's will.

salvation from sin through Christ

Specifically, by saving us Jesus deals with each problem sin raises. Salvation is summarized in Christ's work of justification, adoption, and sanctification. Justification speaks to the legal image of sin. Through Jesus' death on the cross, our offenses against God and his law are atoned. His sacrifice absolved us of guilt and the penalty for sin. He died to satisfy the just requirements of God's law for sin. He died for all sin and for all sinners. To appropriate Christ's atonement, all we need to do is receive it by repentance and faith.

Once justified we are adopted as children of God. Adoption addresses the relational image of sin. Because of sin, we are alienated from God and from each other. Through Christ we are reconciled to God and become his children. At the same time, we are initiated into the church, where we experience reconciliation to humanity, becoming sisters and brothers in Christ. As a redeemed family, we have God as our Father, the Son as our brother, members of the church as siblings, and the Holy Spirit as the source of love. Here, the "dividing wall of hostility" in all human relationships is overcome.

Justification and adoption are what Jesus does *for us* in salvation. However, sanctification is Christ's work *in us*. Sanctification gets to the heart of our problem by purifying us from sin's defilement. Christ not only forgives and reconciles, but he also cleanses us from sin. Christ actually makes us holy. Expressed in the most general terms, sanctification addresses Christ's entire work of transformation in our lives from the moment we are born again until we are glorified in death. The ultimate purpose of sanctification is to make us like Christ so we may be holy as he is holy.

When the Holy Spirit through Christ takes residence in our lives, he begins the process of transforming our attitudes, interests, and actions, while he confronts us with an internal principle of selfishness and sin that persists stubbornly in us. This is called "initial" and "progressive" sanctification. While described in different ways, many Christian traditions believe the Spirit can cleanse this last principle of sin and enable us to love God entirely, to live in complete obedience to his revealed will, and to serve others in love. Terms such as "Christian perfection," "perfect love," "entire sanctification," and "fullness of the Spirit" describe this level of sanctification. As we continue to submit to the Spirit, our love deepens, and our knowledge and understanding of God's will increases, thereby bringing us into greater conformity with Christ until we reach "final sanctification" at death. Therefore, through the work of sanctification we are cleansed from sin, making it possible for us to be brought into full union with God.

where is sanctification?

However, a problem exists in the church. There's a tendency to focus on one part of the problem of sin and Christ's saving work to the neglect of the rest of his work. For example, some of us in the church describe salvation almost entirely in legal terms. Justification becomes the sole focus of redemption. Sure, we acknowledge salvation as more than forgiveness, but we place so much emphasis on forgiveness that we obscure the rest of Christ's saving work. We reduce salvation to a ticket to heaven made possible through Christ's atonement.

Other Christians focus on the relational problems caused by sin. They portray salvation primarily as reconciliation. Through Christ our relationship with God is restored. We become the children of God and friends with Jesus. Salvation is about a new connection with God and growth in intimacy. We often lose sight of the role we played in alienation from God and our need for atonement. We also minimize the necessity of repentance and amendment of life through sanctification.

At times some believers focus so much on sanctification we lose sight of justification and adoption. We are guilty of judging Christians as unbelievers if they struggle to walk in complete obedience to Christ or are unable to live a life free from sin. We believe a Christian's eternal destiny is threatened by the fires of hell if he or she slips up and falls into sin or dies with any unconfessed sin. We forget John's promise to the church: "My dear children, I write this to you so that you will not sin. But if anybody does sin, we have an advocate with the Father—Jesus Christ, the Righteous One. He is the atoning sacrifice for our sins" (1 John 2:1–2).

Christian history provides abundant evidence of believers and churches that have demonstrated a myopic vision of sin and salvation. When not held in balance, the pendulum has swung back and forth between what God does *for us* in salvation and what he does *in us*. Presently, with exceptions, we live in an age in which the church is plagued by a single-minded focus on the legal and relational metaphors. We have reduced salvation to forgiveness of sins or a relationship with God with few demands. Overlooked is the necessity of sanctification. If we are going to be saved from sin, if Jesus is going to be a real Savior, we must emphasize more than justification and adoption. We must be cleansed of sin and experience real sanctification in the present life, even if it is not completed until death.

why forgiveness is not enough

Unfortunately, many of us only want "fire insurance" in salvation. We don't want to go to hell for our sins. Nor do we want to suffer any of sin's consequences. But we don't want to give up sin. We wish to live life on our own terms. We cling to our selfish, sinful, rebellious desires, but we want God to be there to pick up the pieces if our lives fall apart. We want him to rescue us if we fly too close to the flame. We want to try to figure out a way to keep the best part of what we love about sin and remove what we don't. We love our sin more than the kingdom of God. We want the benefits of justification and the privileges of adoption, but we are reluctant to embrace sanctification. We fear holiness will take away what we like best about sin.

A problem arises here. Justification and adoption are not enough to save us without sanctification. Divine forgiveness for sin and reconciliation with God on paper is not enough to redeem us. We must experience real change, the cleansing from sin only Christ's sanctifying work can do. Minimally, there must be a transformation of our desires. We must truly want to turn from our sin, begin to earnestly hunger and thirst for God's righteousness, and turn to Christ for deliverance from sin. We must long to be rid of sin and not just rid of its destructive fruit.

Why is this so? There are at least three reasons, each centering on the holiness of God. The first is obvious. God is a holy God. God is morally good, righteous, and just; this applies to his character, his actions, and his requirements of us. Divine holiness requires atonement for sin and reconciliation, but it also demands amendment of life. We must lead lives that align with God's character and will. Forgiveness of sin through atonement does not bring about the transformation of our character that enables us to reflect God's holiness. Yes, it wipes our slate clean and provides a new beginning, but there must be change in our character that makes us holy as God is holy. Without actual holiness, we will never enter fully into the life of God. We can't even be aligned with God's will.

Second, in final judgment God won't give us what we don't want. If we seek salvation only as fire insurance, it shows our heart's greatest desire. What we really want is our sin and selfishness. We seek our will over God's will; we just don't want to suffer the consequences of sin. We want the pleasures of sin without the pain. The problem is God isn't really going to give us in death what we don't want in the present life. If we pursue sin, he hands us over to it in final judgment. Only those who hunger and thirst to be holy as God is holy are satisfied in the end.

C. S. Lewis reflected on the danger of this predicament well in *The Great Divorce*. Lewis described final judgment as God giving us what we most desire. There is only one ultimate pronouncement in final judgment: "Thy will be done." Either we say it to God or God says it to us. If we desire God's will and God's kingdom above all else in life, we say to God, "Your will be done," and God ushers us into the joy of the Lord. However, if we want sin and our will more than God's, God declares to us, "Thy will be done," and hands us over to our sinful desires.[1] God in final judgment honors us as persons and the formation of our desires in the present life.

Finally, how can we really enjoy the kingdom of God and heaven without a passion for God's holiness? Holiness establishes a life defined by the love of God and the love of neighbor. It is a life of self-giving service to God and others. There is no room for selfish agendas or self-focused living. If we are not made holy, it's impossible for us to enjoy the kingdom of God. If we want to seek a life of self-absorption, self-will, and self-pleasure, how will we be able to enjoy a life in total opposition to it?

Again, C. S. Lewis powerfully illustrated this truth in *The Great Divorce*. He imagined a group of people in hell who receive the opportunity to go to heaven. They are able to experience the delights of heaven and participate in the communion of saints. Our natural inclination is to believe these transplants would be grateful for God's grace and embrace fully their opportunity. Surprisingly, their experience in heaven is dull and uncomfortable. After a few days, they long for their previous lives; they desire to return to hell.[2] Because of the sinful longings of their hearts, because the kingdom of God is so contrary to their desires, they are unsuited for heaven and unable to enjoy paradise.

a brief overview

For us to be saved from sin, God must deal with all the problems of sin. We must experience justification, adoption, and sanctification by God's grace in Jesus Christ. We must experience this work in whole and not in part. While atonement for sin and adoption as God's children must happen, they're not enough. We actually must be changed and transformed. The Bible's teaching through and through is that we must be holy as God is holy (Lev. 20:26; 1 Pet. 1:13–16).

The purpose of this book is to examine "unholiness," the uncleanness that is sin. We want to look at what must be cleansed from our lives in Christ's salvific work. We face two obstacles. Because of sin's pollution, we live in ignorance of our true condition. Only the light of the Holy Spirit through divine revelation can illuminate our spiritual state. Then, when we grasp our condition, we can address unbelief about the extent to which we can be cleansed in the present life. Today's Christian climate is pessimistic about victory over sin. The Holy Spirit must give us faith to believe in Christ's sanctifying work.

A classically biblical way of describing our unholiness is to talk about (a) the flesh, (b) the world, and (c) the Devil. We are corrupted by our flesh under the reign of sin, polluted by the pervasiveness of the world's distorted messages and lies, and defiled by the work of the Devil. If these are threats to our holiness, our pursuit and experience of holiness requires that we know about them and overcome them by Christ's saving grace.

Specifically, chapter 1 reviews the origin of sin and evil. Chapters 2 and 3 examine the flesh and its problems. Chapters 4 and 5 describe the world and its spiritual pollution. Chapters 6 and 7 deal with the problem of the Devil and the demonic and how they prey upon us and lead us into sin. Finally, chapter 8 discusses the resources available to us in our struggle against evil forces that try to get us to sin and become unholy.

1

holy and unholy
THE PROBLEM OF EVIL

So God created mankind in his own image, in the image
of God he created them; male and female he created them.
—Genesis 1:27

They have become filled with every kind of
wickedness, evil, greed and depravity.
—Romans 1:29

Evil is a vexing problem in Christianity. How do we begin to
reconcile the biblical truth of God's omnipotence and supreme
love with the reality of evil? An ancient Greek philosopher named
Epicurus recognized the intellectual problem we face: "The only
way to reconcile God with evil's presence in the world is to deny
one of God's attributes: infinite power or immeasurable goodness.
Either God is all powerful or he is all good, but not both."[1] The
Christian understanding of God appears irreconcilable with evil.

Many Christians point to the beauty and complexity of creation
as testimony to God's existence, power, and goodness. They join
their voices with the psalmist, "The heavens declare the glory of

God; the skies proclaim the works of his hands" (Ps. 19:1). In contrast, David Hume, one of history's best-known atheists, observed the senseless chaos of death, disease, famine, floods, and earthquakes in the physical world combined with the persistence of war, hatred, and unimaginable cruelty in humanity. He concluded, "If there is a God, then the world shows he is a wicked one."[2]

The problem, however, is much deeper than intellectual. On an experiential level, when we see the effects of evil and sin in the world, especially upon the innocent and vulnerable, or when we feel abandoned by God in the midst of tragedy, our souls cry out, "Why, God? If you're a loving God and have control over all existence, why do we suffer?" Platitudes such as "Trust God," "God has a reason for it," or "God will bring good out of it" offer little comfort. We suffer in doubt and fear from what we can't understand.

the problem of evil is central to the biblical story

The problem of evil and sin lies at the very heart of the Bible. From the first book in the Old Testament through the last chapter in the New, we have a clear, well-constructed, overarching narrative with five major plot points: God, creation, fall, redemption, and consummation. The Scriptures begin with recognition of the one true God, who brings the universe into existence out of nothing. Next, the Scriptures vividly describe our first parents' fall into sin and its impact on creation. A lengthy historical account follows. It covers the Father's work of redemption through the call of Israel, through the incarnation of the Son, and through the birth of the church by the Holy Spirit. It culminates when all creation is brought into ultimate union with God. How God redeems the world from evil and makes us incorruptibly holy drives the biblical story.

Many who want to find a logical explanation for evil expressed in formal arguments will be disappointed with the Bible's description. To have the problem of evil addressed through the narrative of Scripture appears insufficient on the surface. They feel like Job, who wanted God to give a clear account of evil and sin. However, God asked Job, "Where were you when I laid the earth's foundation? Tell me, if you understand" (Job 38:4).

Nevertheless, Scripture gives us the story of evil's origin, persistence, and final end. While it may seem unsatisfactory to our modern minds, we live in a world driven by narratives, and they remain the most effective way to communicate God's truth across history and cultures. Only by reflecting on the Christian story does an understanding of evil and sin begin to arise.

In this opening chapter, we want to set the context for the rest of the book by offering historic Christian reflection on the Bible's description of how evil entered into a world created good and holy by God. Let's begin by examining the creation of the universe, followed by the formation of humanity. Next, we will pause to reflect upon God's ultimate purpose for humanity and what God must do to achieve it. We will then discuss the cause of evil in general and conclude with a study of Adam and Eve's original sin in the garden of Eden.

the creation of the universe

The opening chapters of Genesis begin with a depiction of God's creation of the world. As Christians have reflected on it, three major

ideas have emerged relevant to our discussion. First, God brought
the created order into being out of nothing. It's important to emphasize that God created *everything* from *nothing*. Although the Bible
doesn't explicitly use the phrase "out of nothing," the Scriptures
point to this truth. Every part of creation ultimately has its source
and origin in nothing. God didn't use some amorphous substance
that coexisted eternally with him as the building block for creation.
If he did, then matter would be coeternal with God, and God
wouldn't be its creator. Christians recognize God alone is eternal
and uncreated.

God also didn't use his own divine nature as the substance of the
universe. If God's nature was the basis for creation, then the created
order would be divine—it would be God. Christians reject any asser-
tion that the universe is the body of God. Instead, Genesis describes
God as speaking created matter into existence and *then* molding it
into different parts of the world.

Already, we are at a critical point that sets us up for the discussion of evil's origin. The fact that the universe came into being out
of nothing means that all creation is mutable; it's marked by change.
At one time it didn't exist, but suddenly it existed. It moved from
nothing to something. It has change written all over it. To be created
is by definition to be mutable. Therefore, any created substance is
intrinsically mutable, because it has already experienced change and
continues to change through time.

Now mutability isn't necessarily bad. Change can be positive
or negative. Good mutability is seen in growth and development.
We see this in the physical growth of a child, a highway in its construction, a seed in its maturation into a plant, and a young bird
learning to fly. However, mutability can also be bad. We see decline

in our human bodies over time, the destruction of homes by fire, flowers that lose their bloom, and the eventual death of beloved pets.

The question is often asked in theology, "Why didn't God create a world in which sin and evil were impossible?" To begin to answer, we must recognize that God can't create anything that is naturally immutable. Only God's nature is immutable; God's nature doesn't grow; it doesn't become better than it already is; it can't suffer; it can't be harmed; it can't die. This is a fundamental difference between God's uncreated divine nature and the universe's created substance. Our world experiences change because it is created.

Second, God creates out of absolute freedom. There was no need for God to create. Creation didn't have to be. A common question inevitably arises in theology, "Why did God create?" Sometimes we hear responses like "God was lonely and needed someone to love," or "God was bored and needed something to do."

However, answers like these obscure the truth of God's perfection. God isn't dependent upon anyone or anything for his existence, continued existence, or eternal happiness. Furthermore, God is fully realized; there is nothing missing from God, there is no untapped potential in God waiting to be explored. Finally, God isn't lonely, because God is a communion of love among three persons: Father, Son, and Holy Spirit.

Creation, then, is an act of sheer generosity, arising out of God's goodness and self-giving love. It's not about what God gets or what God gains. Creation is about what God gives. God did not become greater or better in the act of creation or by having the universe in existence. There wasn't anything missing in the divine life. God created to share the supreme blessedness of the divine life with others.

While there are clues about God's intentions for creation in Genesis, we don't see fully God's purpose until we get to "consummation" in the biblical narrative, seen in part throughout the story, but clarified in the book of Revelation. The ultimate end of the world is to be brought fully into the life of God and to experience union with him in heaven (Rev. 21–22). We have a foretaste of the "glory to come" through our present union with the Holy Spirit, "who is a deposit guaranteeing our inheritance" to come (Eph. 1:14).

Third, the created order is good. Everything God made is good. At the end of each of the first five days of creation, God judged what he had created as "good." At the end of the sixth day, God declared everything to be "very good." The pronouncement "very good" is God's assessment of human creation on the sixth day, as well as his judgment of all creation. Genesis teaches that God directly created the physical universe with wisdom and purpose. Creation is an expression of divine love. As such, there is nothing inherently evil, sinful, or unspiritual about the created order. Sometimes, because of a latent dualism in Western culture, we can miss the scriptural truth: the world and humanity are good!

the creation of humanity

Genesis describes humanity as the climax of creation. Human beings were God's last creative act before he rested on the seventh day. God "formed man from the dust of the ground and breathed into his nostrils the breath of life, and the man became a living being" (Gen. 2:7). As embodied souls, human beings were also made in the image and likeness of God. The divine image in humanity sets us apart as unique in the world, commanding a dignity and glory unlike that of any other member of creation (Gen. 1:26–27). God placed his stamp of approval, "very good," on our nature as embodied souls and on our place in the world as his image bearers.

We have a basic understanding of what it is for us to be body and soul, but what is it to be created in the image and likeness of God? Historically, the *imago dei* has been interpreted in three complementary ways. First, the divine image encompasses our rational and creative abilities, as well as our moral and affective capacities. As human beings, we have the power to understand the world around us, make sound judgments about it, and act accordingly. Furthermore, like God, who is defined by holiness and love, we are made to reflect God's absolute moral purity by walking in righteousness and to reflect divine love in perfectly ordered affections directed to the love of God and neighbor. As created in the garden, the divine image in Adam and Eve enabled them to act in accordance with sound perception and reason, infused by holy love.

Second, the image of God is found not just in the human individual, not in our moral and rational nature alone, but in our social relationships as well. The Trinity is at the heart of a Christian understanding of God. We do not believe God is a solitary person, but a communion of infinite love among Father, Son, and Holy Spirit. From this perspective, the divine image is not found in the human self only, but in human relationships of self-giving love, mirroring what is expressed between Father, Son, and Holy Spirit. We "image" God in our human communities.

Finally, Genesis explicitly connects humanity's creation in the divine image with the exercise of dominion in the created order. Immediately after the creation of male and female in the image and likeness of God, God gave them the created order to work as stewards. Beyond the rational, moral, and social views, the *imago dei* is seen in what humanity does in the world. As we take responsible care of the world, we reflect God's stewardship of the entire created order. In cultivating, nourishing, and wisely using creation, Adam and Eve embodied the divine image.

John Wesley, in his teaching on Adam and Eve, brought these three views together. He understood the image of God in humanity in the garden to comprise three parts: moral, natural, and political.[3] The moral image enabled humanity to enjoy true righteousness, holiness, love, and knowledge of God in the immediacy of a relationship with God. The natural image gave humanity rationality, understanding, free will, and perfectly ordered affections. The political image furnished humanity with the power of governance, whereby humanity exercised dominion over the created order and walked perfectly in the love of God and neighbor.

As created in the garden before the fall, the divine image enabled human beings to desire, will, and perform perfectly God's intentions for humanity. Holiness, righteousness, and love informed humanity's reasoning, understanding, will, and emotions, which resulted in the wise exercise of stewardship in the created order, rightly ordered relationships with fellow humanity, and perfect love and obedience to God.

created as persons in the image of God

At the center of the three major historic views of the *imago dei* and John Wesley's trifold understanding is the recognition that

Adam and Eve were constituted as persons. To be in the image of God is to be a person, whose identity is formed in relationships. God is a divine community in which each person is identified by his distinctive relationship and interaction with the other persons.

God is Father, Son, and Holy Spirit. This is the very identity of God. The Father is the person of the Father, because he has eternally begotten a Son, has sent the Son to us, and exalts the Son in the world. The Son is the person of the Son because he has a Father from eternity and is distinguished further by his incarnation in obedience to the Father. The Holy Spirit is Spirit because he is eternally "breathed" (*spirated*) by the Father and Son and works to glorify the Father and the Son in creation. Each of the divine persons is who he is because of his distinctive relationships with the other members of the Trinity. Their distinction comes from their relationships.

Through our creation as persons with rational, creative, and moral capacities, forged in the crucible of relationships with God, other human beings, and the world, who exercise stewardship in the created order, we image God, who is a communion or community of persons. Additionally, each part of Wesley's trifold image enables humanity to mirror what takes place in the divine life. Through the moral, natural, and political images, we are able to walk as persons in communion of holy love with God, humanity, and the created order.

the corruptibility and potentiality of humanity in the garden

While made in the image of God in the garden, Adam and Eve were not ultimately where God wanted humanity to be. His goal for us has never been Genesis 1–2, but Revelation 21–22. God's plan

25

"before the foundation of the world" was to bring all of creation into final union with him, described beautifully in the language of marriage and consummation in the New Testament's final chapters. In the end, Christ's saving work is not about returning us to the life Adam and Eve enjoyed before the fall, but about taking us far beyond it.

Even before evil and sin entered the story, God had to address two issues in Adam and Eve if humans were to experience our final purpose: the issues of potentiality and corruptibility. Both arise from the mutability of created natures. The first is potentiality. While made in the image of God, we don't come into life fully formed as persons. Our personhood can be forged only through the relationships and experiences we have in life, as well as through the decisions and choices we make in response to them. They work dynamically to make us who we are.

Adam and Eve were blank slates in the garden and could develop as persons only through their interactive relationships with God, each other, and the world around them. They needed to grow and mature as persons through the exercise of free will and habituating their affections through practice. Only then, as mature persons, could they receive all God had for them in final union in heaven.

Therefore, while Adam and Eve bore God's image in the garden, they were not fully like God yet. God is "pure act." This means God is fully actualized as persons in Father, Son, and Holy Spirit. There is no untapped potential in God. The divine persons do not grow or develop in any way: physically, mentally, emotionally, intellectually, or personally. In contrast, we continue to grow and develop as persons. Because we will be fully actualized as persons in heaven, we will be more like God than Adam and Eve were before the fall. Our first parents needed to develop as persons in the garden.

The second is the issue of corruptibility. Although we are made in the divine image, we are capable of sin. When God created Adam and Eve, he gave them every benefit. Through the *imago dei* the love of God and neighbor came naturally to them, and they were able to relate to the world wisely. Their hearts, minds, and wills were properly ordered. However, because they were created, they were subject to change, both good, as described above, and bad.

God had to deal with the latter. He had to bring humanity to a place where we would be incorruptibly holy, no longer subject to sin, evil, and death. God does this by bringing humanity into full union with him. By being brought fully into the life of God by grace in heaven, humanity will be incorruptible. Because humankind is the creature not the creator (God), incorruptibility will be made possible only through the grace of union.

Here again, Adam and Eve were not yet fully like God. God is incorruptibly holy love. He never does what is contrary to his character. God's freedom isn't what we usually associate with free will. Our natural tendency is to see Adam and Eve's will in the garden as true free will: to have good and evil as real options. However, our first parents had only partial freedom. True freedom is to do only what is in accordance with holy love, as God does. Only when we are fully united with God in heaven will we reflect God in totality. This is why Christian theology has always affirmed that in heaven we will have free will, but sin will not be possible for us. God had to move our first parents from partial to full freedom and make them more fully like himself.

the origin and nature of evil

Now we are at a better place to address the origin and nature of evil and sin. We must begin by making a distinction between moral and natural evil. Moral evil occurs when one *wills* to do what is contrary to God's intentions. Moral evil inflicts harm on the created order. We typically call it sin. Natural evil includes suffering and pain in the world without any personal cause or will behind it. No one decides to make it happen. Some examples include diseases, natural disasters, and accidents. Generally speaking, no one intentionally causes them to happen. They are results of the present state of fallen creation.

How does evil in all forms come about in a world God created as good and holy? Christian theology has offered a threefold response. First, we must recognize that while every part of creation is good, it's mutable. As discussed earlier, going from nothing to something makes change intrinsic to created substances. If the world is mutable, it can change either for better or worse. Sin, pain, and suffering are all an inevitable possibility (but not necessity) of creation.

Second, God made rational creatures, angels, and human beings, and placed them in the world. Like the rest of creation, they are good and holy, but mutable, including their wills. Because their free will is created, it too can change for better or worse. They can exercise their will in alignment with the holy love of God and habituate in righteousness or abuse it. They can depart from the holiness and love in which they were created. We see this take place in the Bible among the angels, with Lucifer and his followers, then in humans with Adam and Eve. Evil entered the world when mutable wills deviated from God's will.

Finally, we recognize that all evil is broken, corrupted, or disordered good. All God has created is good, a declaration made repeatedly by God. Evil occurs when something good is changed for the worse; evil, then, is a corrupted or broken good. As such, evil has no independent existence; it can't exist apart from an intrinsic good, because it is simply a corruption of the good. Therefore behind all evil and sin is something that was originally good.

For example, God created us with the need to eat food to fuel our bodies. He made us to enjoy food as well. However, when the desire for food becomes corrupted in us, it leads to gluttony and other eating disorders. God created sex as a means of procreation and as a pleasurable expression of the most intimate love between husband and wife. However, when our desire for sex becomes broken in us, it causes all kinds of sexual immorality. Furthermore, God made us to love ourselves. We are commanded to love our neighbor as we love ourselves. But when self-love becomes disordered in us, all forms of pride and selfishness arise. In the end, the more broken and corrupted a created nature, action, will, or desire is, the worse it is.

the fall of humanity

Humans were created holy with their wills and affections properly ordered under the reign of the Holy Spirit. However, because humanity was created, we are subject to change: good change that entails growth and development, and bad change that brings corruption, brokenness, and privation.

The story of humanity's fall in the garden is revealing on two levels. First, when the serpent came to tempt Eve, he appealed to good desires in her. As a person created in the image of God, she had the capacity to appreciate beauty. So as the serpent spoke, Eve turned and saw that the fruit from the Tree of Knowledge of Good and Evil was "pleasing to the eye" (Gen. 3:6). The serpent promised if she ate the fruit, she would be "like God" (3:5). Eve had been made for this very purpose. She and Adam bore the image and likeness of God, and were to grow into its fullness. Attraction to the fruit and the desire to be like God were good qualities, but only in the proper economy of God.

The occasion of temptation arose from good and holy desires in Eve that were subject to change; they could fluctuate. The temptation transitioned into sin when those desires became corrupted and disordered. When Eve placed enjoyment of the fruit above her obedience to God's commands, her love became disordered. She loved creation more than the Creator. When she placed the desire to become like God above God himself, her love transitioned from centering on God to a focus on herself. Becoming like God was more important to her than God was.

Second, from Eve's corrupted desires, we can see a sequence of events tracing the corruption of Eve's will. It began with unbelief. The serpent persuaded her to doubt God's earlier warning of death regarding the tree. Unbelief led to pride. Eve thought she knew better than God how to reach her ultimate divine purpose to be fully like God. She thought she had found a better way to happiness than what God had instructed. Pride gave birth to self-will. She determined to put her own will ahead of the will of the One who made her and loved her. Her inward self-will resulted in the outward act of disobedience.

Adam followed Eve's footsteps. The consequences for humanity were devastating. Physical death was set in motion. Although Adam and Eve did not experience physical death immediately, from that time on the human body began to deteriorate, along with the soul, mind, and will. Total corruption of our nature occurs in death. After the fall, the image of God in humanity was left in devastation. Genesis 3–11 paints an ugly picture of its impact. It reversed the original conditions of human life. Morally, humanity became completely dead to God, self-focused, and helpless to change. Naturally, human reason, understanding, and free will became marred, and human affections became inordinate and undisciplined. Politically, humanity's relationship to the world and ability to organize socially was seriously defaced. The natural, moral, and political image of God was replaced with the image of the Devil, defined by pride and self-will.

conclusion

To be fully human is to be holy; to be human is to be as God intended us to be. All sin is a corruption of human nature. The idea "to sin is to be human" is a misunderstanding of what true humanity is. It is because we are not fully human that we sin. The problem of evil is that it makes humanity not fully human.

In the following chapters, we will explore the consequences of the fall, the unholiness resulting from human sin: (1) the corruption of human nature (body, soul, mind, and will) and of the image of God in humanity, leading to disordered human desires and will, resulting in all forms of personal sin (the flesh); (2) the corruption of corporate humanity (the world); and (3) humanity's subjection to the lies, temptations, and bondage to the demonic (the Devil).

2

the flesh
PHYSICAL CORRUPTION

Those who are in the realm of the flesh cannot please God.

—Romans 8:8

The acts of the flesh are obvious: sexual immorality, impurity
and debauchery; idolatry and witchcraft; hatred, discord, jealousy,
fits of rage, selfish ambition, dissensions, factions and envy;
drunkenness, orgies, and the like. I warn you, as I did before, that
those who live like this will not inherit the kingdom of God.

—Galatians 5:19–21

Unfortunately, a form of Gnosticism infects many contemporary
Christians. The Gnostics were heretics in the early church who
believed our physical world, including the human body, is destined
for destruction in the life to come. They believed that only what
is spiritual will exist in heaven. They thought material existence
was at worst intrinsically evil, and at best a divine mistake. Gnostic
salvation, therefore, focused on liberation from the body and birth
into a purely spiritual world.

This heresy manifests itself today in our understanding of human
nature as well. Instead of seeing our nature as unified and whole,
Gnosticism makes divisions and gives greater importance to certain

"parts" over others. It separates our physical and spiritual lives and makes our souls more important than our bodies. It doesn't see how interconnected they are.

the unity of human nature

Historically, Christianity has held three major views of human nature, or what the "substance" is that makes us human. Some theologians have taught that we're purely physical. There's nothing more to us than our bodies. They explain what we call a "spiritual" soul by the physical, biochemical, and neurological processes of the body. The monist perspective (*monist* from the Greek meaning "one") has its foundations in the earliest literature of the Old Testament. It is still dominant in contemporary Judaism. While the apostle Paul used the words *body*, *soul*, and *spirit* to describe our nature (1 Cor. 14:14; 1 Thess. 5:23), Christian monists see these as synonyms used to describe the one physical nature of our bodies.

In contrast, other theologians have picked up on Jesus' distinction between the physical nature of humanity, the body, and the spiritual, the soul (Matt. 10:28; Luke 12:20). The dichotomous view, from the Greek meaning "divided into two parts," believes the soul is a spiritual substance animating and directing the body. In the story of the rich man and Lazarus, Jesus described the state of death as a spiritual existence in which the righteous are at rest at "Abraham's side" and the unrighteous are plagued with regret in torment (Luke 16:19–31). The soul survives death of the body and exists in a conscious state until it is reunited with the body in resurrection at Christ's second coming.

Still other scholars have taken literally the New Testament Epistles' language of "body," "soul," and "spirit" to argue for trichotomous view (Heb. 4:12; 1 Thess. 5:23), which sees our human nature as composed of three elements. In addition to a physical body and a spiritual soul, we also have a spirit, another type of spiritual substance. While the soul is the basis for our rational, emotional, and social capacities, the spirit gives us our religious bent, our spiritual senses. We are able to perceive and respond to God through our human spirit. Through our first parents' disobedience in the garden, we lost our spirit, but have it restored through new birth in Jesus Christ.

Exactly what human nature is remains unresolved and the subject of historic debate theologians and scientists. Nevertheless, the language of "body, soul, mind, and will" or "embodied soul" is commonly used to describe human nature. We talk about our physical body and rational soul without reference to a specific monist, dichotomist, or trichotomist perspective.

There is agreement, however, on the unity of our nature. Regardless of whether humanity is composed of one, two, or three substances, they are intimately connected and affect one another. The physical needs the spiritual, and the spiritual requires the physical. Therefore, we can't be fully human without our entire nature. If any aspect of our nature is missing or corrupted, we're not fully human.

This is why bodily resurrection is central to Christianity. While Western culture, grounded in its ancient Greek roots, has downplayed the importance of the body in human nature's constitution, the Judeo-Christian tradition can't conceive of full humanity apart from the body. To be human is to have a physical body. Physical death, therefore, has always been seen as our enemy.

Make no mistake: although the New Testament indicates a conscious existence for humanity in the intermediate state and our "rest" with Christ in death, as long as the soul is separated from the body, we are less than truly human. All traditional Christian liturgies at funerals point to our ultimate hope: bodily resurrection from the dead at Christ's second coming. Only then will bodily corruption as a consequence of human sin be overcome. If we remain in the state of bodily death, sin and evil have the final word in our lives. This is the apostle Paul's point when he declared, "For if the dead are not raised, then Christ has not been raised either. And if Christ has not been raised, your faith is futile; you are still in your sins. Then those also who have fallen asleep in Christ are lost" (1 Cor. 15:16–18).

the unity of human nature with personhood

Any Christian treatment of our nature's unity must connect it to personhood as well. A simple way to make the distinction between *nature* and *person* is to recognize that nature is "what we have" and person is "who we are." What we have as human beings is a body, soul, mind, and will. We share the same nature in common with all human beings. Whatever it is to be human, each of us has. However, what makes us distinct is our personhood, a unique personhood expressed in each human being. It's the "I" or person behind the particular embodied soul. In the end, we hold the person responsible for the words, thoughts, and actions expressed in each human nature.

While we can draw a distinction between human nature and person, the two are inseparably one and affect each another. Our formation as persons is mediated through our human nature on two levels. On a foundational level, who we are as persons is formed through all our relationships and experiences in the world. When asked who we are, we share the story of our lives—when and where we were born, family relationships, friendships, education, work experiences, and what we enjoy doing for fun. We recognize how collectively these relationships and experiences shape who we are.

Who we are today is a result of the people who have affected our lives in various ways: parents, siblings, teachers, mentors, friends, spouses, bosses, and coworkers. Add into the mix all our experiences: positive, negative, and indifferent. We see clearly the role both people and experiences play in shaping who we are.

On this level, we're more passive in personal formation; our relationships and experiences come to us and shape who we are. On the next level, however, we play an active part in our development through the responses we make to our relationships and experiences. Part of who we are is a result of both deliberate and unconscious decisions we've made. We must include how we've interacted with our parents, friends, teachers, mentors, spouses, and children, as well as the choices we've made in those fork-in-the-road moments. Because we are rational beings, we have a say in who we are and who we become.

How human persons come to be is a dynamic process, both passive and active, mediated through our body, soul, mind, and will. Human nature is the medium through which we receive and direct. Who we are as persons is forged in the crucible of life, and our embodied soul is the medium.

For example, Martha and Joann share the same nature. Each has a human body, soul, mind, and will. This is what makes them human. However, they are distinct persons; they are distinguishable subjects, and each is a one-of-a-kind expression of human nature.

Martha was born in rural Arkansas to rice-farming parents in the 1950s. She came to adulthood during the turbulence of the Vietnam War and the sexual revolution era. She married her high school sweetheart with whom she has three daughters.

Joann, on the other hand, was born to steel mill workers in Pittsburgh, Pennsylvania, in the 1970s. She experienced the precipitous decline of the metal industry and its impact upon her family. After high school, she studied business at Carnegie Mellon University and pursued a career in banking. She married, but after a brief time she left her husband because he had an affair. She has never had children.

While Martha and Joann are human beings, their relationships and experiences, as well as their decisions, have been different, shaping them into the unique individual persons they are. Their human nature is the means by which they became who they are today and who they will become in the future.

the flesh: corrupted human nature and personhood

In contrast to Gnosticism, which separates the body and soul and sees the soul as good and the body as bad, historic Christianity portrays human nature and human personhood as a unified whole created in the moral, natural, and political image of God in the garden. Through the disobedience of our first parents, however, the divine image in humanity has been corrupted; our nature and personhood have been injured.

Christian theology describes our corruption in a number of ways: brokenness, diminishment, or privation. Corruption, however, isn't a "thing" added to us like a contagion, infection, or substance. It is the loss of full expression of the *imago dei* in our nature and personhood. Brokenness conveys the damage sustained to God's image in us, causing dysfunction. Diminishment communicates its deterioration, while privation speaks of its loss.

Let's use the example of a winter coat to illustrate. To say the coat is corrupted, as we're using the term, doesn't mean it has become dirty from playing outside. Dry mud doesn't keep it from being a coat, nor does it interfere with its intended purpose: to keep its owner warm and protected from the weather. However, if the coat is broken in two, torn in half, its purpose is threatened unless someone sews it back together. If the coat wears away gradually through use, its material becomes thin, and eventually becomes too diminished to protect against the elements. The same is true if the coat develops holes through rough play and becomes increasingly privated of the cloth that makes it a coat. In each instance, nothing is added detrimentally to the coat; it only experiences different forms of deterioration.

Our most basic problem as human beings is the corruption, brokenness, diminishment, or privation of our nature and personhood. The New Testament calls the corrupted divine image in us the "flesh" to express human nature and personhood under the reign of sin (Rom. 8:4–9; Gal. 5:17). In other passages, Paul referred to it as "the flesh" or sinful nature (Rom. 8:3, 5, 8), our "worldly" condition (1 Cor. 3:1), and the "law of sin" (Rom. 7:23). Our human bodies, souls, minds, and wills are corrupted. This is our nature under the reign of sin.

The flesh is manifested in human life through the moral, natural, and political image of God expressed in our nature and personhood. For the rest of the chapter, our focus will be on the flesh as seen in the corrupted moral and natural image. Because the political image relates to corporate humanity, we will discuss it in greater detail in our treatment of the world.

the corrupted moral image

Christ summarized life's primary purpose in the two Great Commandments. We are commanded to love God with all our being and to love our neighbor as ourselves (Matt. 22:37–40). We glorify God and experience joy when we walk in love. The moral image of God, as created in the garden, properly directed all human desires and inclinations toward our ultimate purpose. Godly love and holiness informed all human thought, understanding, judgment, and action.

We must ask at this point, "What is love?" Biblically and theologically, love is composed of two inseparable parts: (1) the desire for union or fellowship with another and (2) the decisions and actions to bring it about. For example, if we say we love our family, we express our desire to be with them and to be in healthy relationships. It also means we make consistent life choices that promote fellowship. Without both, we don't have the full expression of love. We see this all too often in marriages—husbands and wives who desire to be with each other, but then allow career pursuits or outside commitments to get in the way of their relationship. Their choices end up betraying their desire, and love falters.

We are able to see holiness now more clearly as well. When we say, "God is holy," we speak of the absolute moral purity of God in character and action. But what exactly is "moral purity"? Simply put, it's what love demands for true union in relationship. Holiness incorporates the dispositions, choices, and actions demanded for full fellowship.

For example, if a young man's father has emotionally abused him, but he loves his father, he desires reconciliation. Real love, however, isn't simply forgiveness, although forgiveness is a start. For true fellowship to be restored, the father must repent and amend his behavior. If the father balks, then reconciliation can't take place. The son's love must be holy, he must make decisions and choices that lead to his father's repentance and full reconciliation, not settling for just the appearance of reconciliation. Holiness demands what love requires in a healthy relationship between father and son.

Love is demonstrated supremely in the triune life of God shared by Father, Son, and Holy Spirit, in which each person in the Trinity desires union with the other persons and wills that fellowship in holiness. To confess that "God is love" is to recognize God as a divine community of persons who give themselves in holy love to one another. As human beings created in the moral image of God in the garden of Eden, our desires were established in holy love. We wanted above all else fellowship with God, neighbor, and the created order, as well as the holiness required for such union.

Because of utter devastation to the moral image of God in us through the fall, humanity was left spiritually bankrupt, self-focused, and helpless to change. The desire for divine union and the holiness required for it have shifted. As human beings, we haven't quit longing for union, but the object of our union has shifted. We have exchanged the supreme love of God and the love of neighbor for the love of ourselves and creation. We love creation rather than the Creator.

Christian theologians have described the corruption of the moral image in two related ways: humanity's disordered love and its propensity to sin. As we have seen, everything God has created is good, and God has formed us to be social beings in multifaceted relationships. Through these relationships, our personhood is forged. Only when we love God supremely can all other loves or relationships be rightly ordered. Our love for God properly directs all other loves, so that we appropriately desire relationships with people, ourselves, and creation. However, with the moral image corrupted in us, our loves become disordered and inordinate. Without the supreme love of God directing our lives, chaos reigns in our relationships.

John Chrysostom, an early church father, described our problem well in his teaching on our first parents. After Eve was formed and brought to Adam, the Scriptures state they were "both naked, and they felt no shame" (Gen. 2:25). After they ate the forbidden fruit, however, they became naked and ashamed (3:7, 10–11). Chrysostom asked, "What caused their change in attitude toward nakedness?" Before their disobedience, he answered, Adam and Eve were so focused on the "other" they didn't take notice of themselves.[1] With the moral image of God fully formed in them, they loved God supremely and gave themselves in full love to their spouse and to creation. Even their self-love was formed by the love they received from God and their spouse. After the moral image was corrupted by the fall, their attention turned inward. They became self-focused and realized their nakedness for the first time. Without the supreme love of God properly directing all other loves, Adam and Eve's love became disordered, focused unhealthily on themselves and other parts of creation.

Scholars also picture humanity's corrupted moral image as a bent or propensity toward rebellion, disobedience, and selfishness in life. We balk at the love for God and neighbor. Instead of being good stewards of the created order, its exploitation for selfish gain is what comes naturally to us. Living the virtuous life, doing what's right, comes only with great struggle, if at all. When push comes to shove, when the rubber hits the road, when our best intentions meet the realities of life, our sinful tendencies rise to the surface, no matter how hard we try to suppress them.

One way to glimpse the sinful orientation of our hearts is to observe what we think, say, or do when we believe no one is watching. It's manifested in the secret thoughts we never share with others or in our offensive words spoken off the record, because we wouldn't want them to be made public. We may suppress our corrupted impulses when we are in the light, but when the cover of darkness comes, the propensity of our heart surfaces.

Both disordered love and a sinful propensity are manifestations of the corrupted moral image. We also call this privation "original sin," because it's one of the major ways we suffer the consequences of our first parents' disobedience. It is also called the "nature" of sin, because sin directs us at the very center of our being.

the corrupted natural image

If the moral image establishes our desire for God and neighbor, then the natural image empowers us to know what love requires for real union and to align our will with it. The natural image of God in Adam and Eve enabled them to know what holy love requires in all relationships and to walk accordingly. They were capable of looking at the world and knowing intuitively what needed to be done in every instance. They were then able to make it happen through the exercise of their will.

After the natural image's corruption in the fall, vestiges of human rationality remained, but our understanding and judgment became clouded. We no longer see clearly the world in which we live. Confusion reigns. Furthermore, even when we know what the love of God and neighbor requires, we struggle to do it. We lack the strength of will to act accordingly. We therefore have two areas that are compromised in complications from the diminished natural image: understanding and exercising the will.

First, humanity lacks the knowledge, wisdom, and understanding to walk fully in the supreme love of God and neighbor. We look at the world around us and recognize our perceptions and judgments about it are limited or mistaken. Even if the human heart were properly oriented and the mind had complete power of the will, restrictions in understanding and judgment would lead to mistakes in every area of human relationship. We would desire to do what's right and have the will to do it, but we wouldn't have clarity about what needed to be done. The problem is we see "through a glass darkly."

Because of the moral image's corruption, humanity has lost the immediacy of a relationship with God. Apart from God's grace, we have no knowledge of God or his requirements for us. Even when the Holy Spirit gives divine revelation to human conscience or direction through the Scriptures, we wrestle in discerning what it means and in how exactly to apply it in life.

We struggle also in knowing what's best in our relationships with the people we love most. Husbands may love their wives and want to honor them but struggle in knowing how to respond appropriately when problems arise in the marriage. Parents make poor decisions raising their children, even though they're acting in what they believe is their children's best interest. Friends give poor advice to one another, even though they try to offer wise counsel. The human heart and will aren't the problem in these cases; human understanding and judgment are.

Our diminished rationality leads to errors in judgment in all human relationships. We call these mistakes in Christianity "sins of infirmity," because they are unintentional and arise from a shortcoming in human reasoning. They're sin because they cause humanity to fall short of the perfect will of God in relationships with him, others, and the created order. They're sin because they cause harm in our relationships.

Second, humanity has a problem with exercising the will. Because of the natural image's brokenness, our will balks at the demands of the supreme love of God and neighbor. When we know God's desires, we resist them at the level of will. In *Confessions*, Augustine of Hippo observed the problem our human will encounters when God's command confronts it:

The mind gives an order to the body and is at once obeyed, but when it gives an order to itself, it is resisted. What causes it? The mind commands the hand to move and is so readily obeyed that the order can scarcely be distinguished from its execution. Yet the mind is mind and the hand is part of the body. But when the mind commands the mind to make an act of the will (e.g., to forgive enemy), these two are one and the same and yet the order is not obeyed. The mind orders itself to make an act of the will, and it would not give this order unless it willed to do so; yet it does not carry out its own command.[2]

The human will balks at the demands of holy love through defiance and weakness. Our will cries in rebellion, "I won't," to the will of God. At this point, it conspires with our corrupted desires. We may know what God wants from us, and we may have insight about what we need to do in love, but our will refuses to submit to God's commands. It asserts itself in opposition to the good. It's hostile to holy love.

If the human will surrenders its rebellion, it succumbs to weakness. It cries out in defeat, "I can't," to God's directions. There is some desire to do the will of God here, but the will is weak. It can't follow through. "The spirit is willing, but the body is weak" (Matt. 26:41). Paul described our problem in Romans 7:22–23: "For in my inner being I delight in God's law; but I see another law at work in me, waging war against the law of my mind and making me a prisoner of the law of sin at work within me."

Christian theology has called the human will's stubbornness and weakness, "the power of sin" in human life. We recognize the good we're called to do and the sin we need to avoid, but we're incapable of walking in the light God has given us. No matter how hard we try, sin has dominion over our will.

Three categories of sin are associated with our fallen will: (a) intentional sin, (b) habitual sin or strongholds of sin, and (c) sins of surprise. Unlike sins of infirmity, where ignorance is the issue, the problem here is a lack of resolve. Intentional sins are deliberate and willful. We intentionally transgress a known law of God. We don't want to walk in obedience to the light God has given us. We choose our will over God's. The power to obey is in us, but we simply choose otherwise.

Habitual sin or strongholds of sin are compulsive behaviors that we regularly commit, over which we have little or no control in life.

We often call them addictions. We can sense their seductive pull and feel their power grow in us until we fall helplessly into their clutches. Even if we recognize their destructive consequences, we have little strength to resist them. The problem with our will now is not defiance but weakness.

Finally, there are sins of surprise. They're not willful like intentional sin; they're not addictive behaviors and don't give obvious clues to their approach like habitual sin. Rather, they seize us in the moment before we've had a chance to think about them. We weren't planning them, and we really didn't choose to do them; we committed them without thinking.

For example, in the heat of the moment we may utter a curse word under our breath without thinking. We rarely, if ever, curse. We didn't plan or want to say it, but we spoke it before we even realized it. Also, we may go through a period in life with high anxiety, caused by too many commitments and responsibilities coupled with problems in our most important relationships. When a coworker speaks a slight word of criticism, we explode in ungodly anger. We normally don't struggle with such anger; we didn't see it coming, but it happened without our thinking. These are sins that surprise us.

conclusion

The apostle Paul warned repeatedly about the problems of the flesh. Those who live in "the flesh" can't please God, and they live in danger of being excluded from Christ's kingdom (Gal. 5:19–21). If we're going to be saved, God must deliver us from the flesh.

The flesh is the corrupted moral and natural image of God in humanity expressed in human nature and personhood. It's our embodied souls under the reign of sin. Salvation requires the restoration of our moral image by the grace of Jesus Christ. The supreme desire for fellowship with God must be renewed in us, thereby aligning all other loves in life. Our heart's propensity to selfishness and disobedience also must be corrected so that holiness defines our disposition.

Redemption also demands a renovation of the natural image. We need to have knowledge, wisdom, and understanding from God so we can discern clearly what the love of God and neighbor requires in relationship. More importantly, however, we need Christ to crush our rebellious will and the Holy Spirit to fortify our will so we can walk in holy love, bringing victory over intentional, habitual, and surprise sins.

3

the flesh's problems
and its implications

For we know that our old self was crucified with him so that the
body ruled by sin might be done away with, that we should no longer be
slaves to sin. . . . Therefore do not let sin reign in your mortal body so
that you obey its evil desires. Do not offer any part of yourself to sin
as an instrument of wickedness, but rather offer yourselves to God
as those who have been brought from death to life; and offer
every part of yourself to him as an instrument of righteousness.

—Romans 6:6, 12–13

"All sin is the same in the eyes of God. No matter how big or
small your sin is, it's the same to God."

In the church the idea that all sin is the same in God's eyes is
common. It pervades contemporary evangelicalism. Whether
through sermons, Sunday school classes, Bible studies, or friendly
conversations with other Christians, we pick up the idea quickly.
While Christians may be ignorant of Christian doctrine's finer
points, everyone knows how God views sin. To question this truth
is to invite immediate disbelief and suspicion.

The rationale for such teaching varies. In an attempt to exalt the
holiness of God, some Christians try to show how even the smallest

infraction of God's law is as bad as the greatest infraction before God's absolute moral purity. Others argue, if all sin has the same punishment (death) as some biblical passages appear to suggest, then every sin is the same to God. And some believers claim that because sin has the same impact on our relationship with God (separating us from God and requiring the sacrificial death of Christ to forgive) all sins must be equal in God's sight.

However, generally speaking, no major Christian theologian or historic Protestant, Roman Catholic, or Eastern Orthodox tradition believes all sin is equal in God's eyes. It exists only as folk theology, a belief uncritically held by laity and preachers. Unfortunately, our evangelical folk theology has serious consequences when dealing with the problems of the flesh.

levels and degrees of sin in the eyes of God

A well-known example of Christian teaching on levels and degrees of sin is the Roman Catholic distinction between mortal and venial sins. Mortal sins are so serious that they lead to the perpetrator's spiritual death if they continue without amendment of life. Venial sins, in contrast, are "light"; they don't harm irreparably a person's relationship with God. Mortal sins are to be avoided at all costs, and venial sins are to be worked on through sanctification.

Unfortunately, often the idea of some sins being worse than others in God's eyes is quickly dismissed as "That's what Roman Catholics believe." However, every major historical expression of Christianity has recognized there are levels and degrees of sin before God. This classic Christian understanding of sin is captured well in the Reformed/Presbyterian tradition's "Westminster Larger Catechism":

Q. 150. Are all transgressions of the law of God equally heinous in themselves, and in the sight of God?

A. All transgressions of the law are not equally heinous; but some sins in themselves, and by reason of several aggravations, are more heinous in the sight of God than others.

Q. 151. What are those aggravations that make some sins more heinous than others?

A. Sins receive their aggravations,

1. From the persons offending; if they be of riper age, greater experience or grace, eminent for profession, gifts, place, office, guides to others, and whose example is likely to be followed by others.

2. From the parties offended: if immediately against God, his attributes, and worship; against Christ, and his grace; the Holy Spirit, his witness, and workings; against superiors, men of eminency, and such as we stand especially related and engaged unto; against any of the saints, particularly weak brethren, the souls of them, or any other, and the common good of all or many.

3. From the nature and quality of the offence: if it be against the express letter of the law, break many commandments, contain in it many sins: if not only conceived in the heart, but breaks forth in words and actions, scandalize others, and admit of no reparation: if against means, mercies, judgments, light of nature, conviction of conscience, public or private admonition, censures of the church, civil punishments;

and our prayers, purposes, promises, vows, covenants, and engagements to God or men: if done deliberately, willfully, presumptuously, impudently, boastingly, maliciously, frequently, obstinately, with delight, continuance, or relapsing after repentance.

4. From circumstances of time, and place: if on the Lord's day, or other times of divine worship; or immediately before or after these, or other helps to prevent or remedy such miscarriages: if in public, or in the presence of others, who are thereby likely to be provoked or defiled.[1]

Because this is a catechism, an instructional manual for young people preparing to be confirmed in their faith, it's not meant to be exhaustive. It simply outlines major ways in which some sins are "more heinous" in God's eyes than others. While not all would agree with every specific example cited, the general rationale offered is in agreement with historic Christian teaching.

The Eastern Orthodox tradition of Christianity makes similar distinctions when reflecting on what makes some sins worse than others. The sin itself, motivation behind the sin, the age and maturity of the person who committed it, how many times it was done, and the manner in which it was done are taken into consideration in the evaluation of the severity of acts of sin.[2]

Additionally, there are at least five other major biblical and theological reasons for the church's historic stance on sin.

strong biblical foundations

The Bible repeatedly shows some sins being worse before God than others. While there is not enough space to walk through all biblical evidence in this book, here are a couple of clear examples. First, God clearly sees intentional sin as more serious than unintentional sin. In the holiness code given by God to Israel in Leviticus 1–17, God made a clear distinction between intentional sin and unintentional sin. The sacrificial system was able to atone only for unintentional sin. There was no atonement offered for intentional sin. Intentional sin was punishable by death. Again, God made a clear distinction between intentional and unintentional sin—one could be atoned for through the sacrificial system; the other could not. The foundations of the holiness code remain today in the Jewish observance of Yom Kippur, the Day of Atonement, through which unintentional sins are forgiven, but intentional sins are not.

This basic idea and distinction carries over into the New Testament as well, as seen in the apostle Paul's instruction in the book of Romans. In Romans 6:23, he declared, "For the wages of sin is death." While many quote Paul here to argue for all sin being the same in God's eyes because it carries the same punishment, the context reveals otherwise. The apostle was writing to believers. He was warning Christians: "The wages of sin is death." In the larger setting of Romans 6, Paul was teaching followers of Jesus that they didn't have to sin (vv. 1–2, 15) and in the end they must not sin, because "the wages of sin is death" (v. 23).

More specifically in Romans, Paul had a very clear operating definition of sin—a deliberate transgression of the known law of God. He was not writing about unintentional sin or sins of ignorance. He began the book by addressing the Gentiles. He said they had been given a law to follow: the law of conscience. They, nevertheless, had chosen not to follow this internal law, and God had handed them over to judgment as a result (Rom. 1:18–32). Paul then turned to the Jews (2:17—3:23). They had received a written law. Still, they had intentionally broken the written law. His teaching culminated with Romans 3:23: "For all have sinned." Both Gentile and Jew had received a law that they deliberately disobeyed. Paul's point in Romans 6:23 was to warn Christians of the dangers of an intentional transgression of a known law of God, not sin committed unintentionally or in ignorance. And Paul earlier implied that sins of ignorance weren't really counted as sin: "To be sure, sin was in the world before the law was given, but sin is not charged against anyone's account where there is no law" (5:13).

The writer of Hebrews picked up the teaching found in the Old Testament's holiness code in 10:26–27. The main thrust of the letter is an exhortation for the church to persevere in their faith, lest they fall and not make it to the Promised Land (Heb. 5:11—6:12). While Christ is a greater priest, who makes a superior sacrifice for sin in a better sanctuary than the temple (7:1—10:18), Christians are warned, if they continue in intentional sin, there is no sacrifice that can atone for their sin—not even the blood of Jesus. Again, God makes a clear distinction between intentional and unintentional sin. Intentional sin is far more serious and spiritually dangerous than the other.

Second, sins are judged differently by God and the believing community in both the Old and New Testaments. A clear example of God's contrasting evaluation of sin is the tour God gave Ezekiel of the sins of Israel. God showed Ezekiel four scenes of abomination with each being a greater offense to God as they move from the outskirts of Jerusalem to the center of the temple. God began by showing Ezekiel an "idol that provokes jealousy" at the north gate (Ezek. 8:3–6). Even worse to the Lord were seventy elders offering incense to idols at the entrance to the temple's courtyard (vv. 7–13). Still worse were women who wept for the god Tammuz at the north gate of the temple, a Babylonian ritual of mourning. Instead of worshiping a living God, they lamented the dead (vv. 14–15). The final and supreme act of idolatry took place in the inner court of the temple, where twenty-five men turned their backs to the temple in rejection of worshiping Yahweh and faced the east to worship the sun (v. 16). Each of these four abominations was directly against God. God personally assessed each abomination and judged all of them to be a succession of increasing depravity. Combined with Israel's sins against humanity, they had provoked God's wrath (v. 17).

In the New Testament, greater and lesser sins are seen in how they are addressed. Jesus warned the religious leaders about an unpardonable sin. Blasphemy of the Son of God can be forgiven, but blasphemy against the Holy Spirit can't (Matt. 12:22–32). Paul instructed the Corinthian church to excommunicate a young man because he was sleeping with his stepmother (1 Cor. 5:1–5), while the grumblers in the community received only a warning (9:24—10:13). Similarly, Paul disciplined Hymenaeus and Alexander by handing them "over to Satan to be taught not to blaspheme" through their teaching of false doctrine (1 Tim. 1:18–20). He warned the Galatian churches about the "acts of the sinful nature," stating that "those who live like this will not inherit the kingdom of God" (Gal. 5:21). And John distinguished between Christians engaging in sins that lead to death and sins that don't (1 John 5:16–17).

different metaphors for sin

The Bible uses multiple metaphors in its teaching about sin. Too often in evangelicalism, we look at sin only from a legal perspective. We see it only as a transgression of God's law. The Scriptures, however, describe sin in relational/familial (alienation, estrangement, breaking of covenant relationship) and worship/temple (clean and unclean) metaphors as well. Sin isn't just legal; it has relational and purity concerns attached to it. We must view sin in the light of its impact on people's relationships with God, each other, and creation, as well as the degree to which it defiles and corrupts people.

During the Second World War, Corrie ten Boom and her Christian family hid Jews fleeing Nazi persecution in their home in Amsterdam, Netherlands. One of the ethical dilemmas Corrie faced was whether to lie about their presence when SS officers came to inquire about the family harboring Jews. Corrie was convinced telling any falsehood was a sin against the command of God. She decided, however, in this case lying was necessary to protect the Jews.

While it may be argued that she sinned in a legal sense by telling the Nazi officers her family didn't hide any Jews, there were other issues at play. Relationally, her lie was an attempt to save other people. She was not attempting to cover up the fact that she was a Christian and denying Christ. She wasn't trying to save her own life. Love of God and love of the Jews moved her to lie.

Furthermore, it didn't corrupt Corrie. Her deceit didn't lead to a spiraling descent into even more sin. Instead, it led to greater commitment to serve God and the Jews. To have a holistic view of sin, as the Bible and historic Christianity does, we must go beyond simply looking at sin only in terms of legality.

We see the relational nature of sin in a number of places in the Bible. After the Israelites made the golden calf, Moses accused them of committing a "great sin" (Ex. 32:30). The calf represented a common god in the ancient Near East that the Egyptians worshiped. The Israelites were reverting back to a prior and common form of worship. They were doing what they had always done. What made their sin more grievous was the violation of their covenant relationship with God. They had committed formally to serve and worship only Yahweh (Ex. 19). To worship the golden calf after the covenant at Sinai was worse than when they were in Egypt, because at Sinai they had a different relationship with God.

Jesus recognized the relational nature of sin in his words to Pilate: "The one who handed me over to you is guilty of a greater sin" (John 19:11). Judas was guilty of a worse sin than Pilate, because Judas was Jesus' friend who had followed him for three years. Pilate had just met Christ. Both Judas and Pilate sinned against Christ, but Judas's sin was worse because of his relationship with Jesus.

The Bible also shows defilement caused by sin. Jesus recognized and acknowledged that the Pharisees kept the letter of the law. Their problem with sin wasn't legal; it was internal. They were defiled by sin. Their problem didn't involve their obedience to the law of God but the corruption of their hearts. Jesus stated, "Woe to you, teachers of the law and Pharisees, you hypocrites! You are like whitewashed tombs, which look beautiful on the outside but on the inside are full of the bones of the dead and everything unclean. In the same way, on the outside you appear to people as righteous but on the inside you are full of hypocrisy and wickedness" (Matt. 23:27–28).

For example, if a husband tells a white lie to his wife about the dress she's wearing, saying it looks beautiful on her when he thinks actually it's unflattering, in his dishonesty he commits a legal sin. His lie will most likely have some impact on their relationship as well. However, the husband's lie isn't nearly as damaging to their relationship as the sin of adultery or physical abuse. While both lying and adultery are legal sins, their consequences in the degree to which they corrupt the marriage relationship are different.

In the end, Scripture doesn't look at sin simply from a legal perspective, but also from the degree to which it harms relationships and corrupts people. These are factors in God's judgment of sin.

levels and degrees of corruption

Sin is evaluated by the degree to which something has fallen from its original goodness and intended purpose. Everything God has created is good. Behind any sin is ultimately something good. Sin is the expression of a corrupted or broken good. The more sin strips away the original goodness, however, the worse it is. Because God is the creator of the good, he is fully aware of the degree to which it has been corrupted.

We must grasp two ideas here: (1) Behind any sin is a "good" created by God, and (2) sin manifests various degrees of the corrupted good. First, while it may seem counterintuitive, all sin is corruption of something that God created as good. We recognize, for example, that God has made humanity in such a way that we require food and drink to sustain life. He has also made us to enjoy food, enabling us to experience great pleasure from it. We were created to eat and enjoy food. This is good. Yet when the desire to eat and enjoy food becomes broken in us, it leads to different types of sin, ranging from gluttony on one hand to anorexia on the other.

We see this truth in sex as well. God created us male and female for the purpose of procreation. Without sexual relations, humanity would cease to exist. But there is more to human sex than reproduction. God has made humanity to experience pleasure in the giving and receiving of love between a husband and wife in sexual relations. It is a sign or pointer to the union between Christ and his church at the end of human history. Sex is good. However, when the sexual drive within us becomes broken, it brings about different forms of sexual sin in thought and deed: lust, pornography, promiscuity, polygamy, adultery, and so forth.

The same is true of love of oneself. God formed us to love ourselves. Jesus said, "Love your neighbor as yourself" (Matt. 22:39). A part of self-love is the desire for self-preservation, seen in the garden of Gethsemane, when Jesus prayed for the cup of crucifixion and death to pass from him (26:36–46). Nevertheless, when the love of self becomes corrupted in us, it leads to pride and selfishness on one hand and self-loathing and hatred on the other. Jesus avoided both extremes in his full surrender to the will of the Father and his embrace of the cross.

Second, every sin reveals different degrees of corruption; the more something has been stripped of its original goodness, the worse sin it is in God's eyes. Some sins express greater degrees of "fallenness" from the original goodness God created. Rape is worse than consenting sex between a man and woman who aren't married. Why? Because sex between a consenting male and female more closely approximates the original design of sex between husband and wife than rape does. While both are sinful, one is more so because it expresses a greater corruption of the original good of sex, in addition to the violence perpetrated against the victim.

To begin to think in this way, begin with the original good: sex is the manifestation of self-giving love between a man and woman in the covenant of marriage, where focus is given to the other spouse and each one finds completion or union in the other. While there is more "good" in marital sexual relations than stated here, most Christian theologies would agree on this being one of marriage's divinely ordained purposes. Next, think of the most corrupted or depraved expressions of sex: perhaps incest or molestation of a child. At this point, you have begun to construct a spectrum from best to worst. Now to fill in the spectrum, begin to think of increasing degrees of corruption.

For example, a husband may have sex with his wife for his own personal gratification. While this is acceptable in marriage and a reason Paul exhorted some Christians to get married (1 Cor. 7:9), a degree of corruption has entered into the sexual relationship. Sex is no longer a focus on the other spouse. Worse still is the case of a spouse seeking her own gratification through pornography. She is intended to find sexual completion in her husband, but instead finds it outside her husband through fantasy. Even greater corruption enters the picture when the spouse seeks sex with another partner and the marriage covenant is broken completely. From here sexual sin continues a downward spiral to the most depraved sexual sins, ones far removed from sex's original good.

This exercise can be done with any sin. While there may be some disagreements about what the original good is and what its most corrupted expression might be, we can imagine it. Knowingly and unknowingly, individual churches and denominations work with this understanding of sin when they "draw lines in the sand" about what is acceptable and unacceptable in the lives of their members and leaders. God, however, who has created everything good, is fully aware of the degree to which sin has stripped something of its original goodness.

sin on pastoral and practical levels

On a pastoral level, saying all sin is the same in the eyes of God doesn't work. On a theological level, if we're not careful, we can make God look like a monster. Sometimes, in our attempt to elevate the absolute holiness of God and our problem with sin, we portray God in unhelpful ways or we risk trivializing real depths of depravity in the world. A parent who mistakenly offers loving advice to his or her children but leads them astray from the perfect will of God is not the same to God as Adolf Hitler murdering six million Jews. The latter sin is far worse than the former. To say they are the same is to misrepresent the God revealed to us in Jesus Christ. Jesus rebuked the Pharisees for being so focused on the minor details of God's law that they missed "the more important matters" like justice, mercy, and the needs of others (Matt. 23:23).

On a practical level, teaching all sin is the same in God's eyes can undermine wise pastoral counsel. Imagine a young Christian woman struggling with homosexual desire and seeking counsel from a spiritual mentor. Because she thinks all sin is the same to God—to have homosexual thoughts, to read homosexual erotic literature, and to fantasize sexually is just as bad as engaging in actual sex—she has decided to give in and have sex with another woman. If all sin is the same and thinking it is as bad as doing it, there is little to offer by way of practical exhortation. However, if historic Christian teaching is correct, she has been misled in her understanding. She needs to understand how acting on her sin is far worse than simply thinking about it or desiring it.

At this point, Jesus' teaching on thoughts and actions in the Sermon on Mount is brought up to counter such historic Christian reasoning and counsel given here. Jesus declared, "You have heard that it was said to the people long ago, 'Do not murder, and anyone who murders will be subject to judgment.' But I tell you that anyone who is angry with a brother or sister will be subject to judgment" (Matt. 5:21–22). Likewise, "But I tell you that anyone who looks at a woman lustfully has already committed adultery with her in his heart" (v. 28).

In the larger extended passage (vv. 20–48), Jesus was teaching that God is not just concerned with outward conformity to the law, but inward conformity as well. Jesus began by saying his audience's righteousness must exceed that of the Pharisees and the teachers of the law (v. 20). The Pharisees kept the law outwardly, but not inwardly. Jesus' point, however, wasn't that inward conformity and outward action are equal. His point was that God wants inward conformity. Jesus' more specific teaching on anger (vv. 21–22) and lust (vv. 27–28) were in the context of a number of hyperbolic statements, including the most famous: "If your right eye causes you to stumble, gouge it out. . . . If your right hand causes you to stumble, cut it off and throw it away" (vv. 29–30). In other words, while Jesus was saying that ungodly anger toward someone is the same as murder and lust is the same as actually committing adultery, he didn't mean it literally. Just as we see in his instruction about gouging out an eye or severing an arm, this is Jesus using hyperbole to make the point that God is concerned about our intentions, but thinking something is not literally the same as doing it.

The all-or-nothing mentality of "sin is sin" can stunt genuine progress in the process of sanctification. Often Christians improve in one area of their lives without having complete victory in it. To say all sin is the same risks denying the growth that has taken place and the encouragement accompanying it. It is a positive step forward when an alcoholic stops drinking, even if he still desires to get drunk or when a person who struggles with anger management no longer lashes out at friends and coworkers, even if she thinks about doing so. It is a positive step forward when a gossip stops talking in unflattering ways about others, even though he continues to imagine doing so. We Christians aren't where we need to be, but we are more like Christ than we were. Sometimes, as we pray and counsel other believers, we just want to see them take the next step toward full victory over a particular sin.

all sin may not have the same punishment

One of the primary arguments made for the equality of sin is that it has the same punishment—death/hell. However, such rationale is guilty of the logical fallacy of division. This fallacy happens when a person reasons that something true of the whole must be true for all its parts. For example, the Willis Tower in Chicago is heavy. Therefore, every nail, brick, and beam is equally heavy. Here it is easy to recognize the fallacy.

Because sin has the same punishment (what is true of the whole), all sin must be the same in God's eyes (not true). The church has made the distinction between punishment and degrees of sin. The fact that sin may (or may not) have the same punishment does not necessarily mean that all sin is the same in the eyes of God. Adolf Hitler's genocide and an individual murdering another person in revenge for an attack on a family member would have the same punishment in the state of Texas. It doesn't make the crimes the same in degree. One is greater than the other on many levels—not just from a human perspective, but from the divine perspective as well. God is fully aware of all of the consequences of the two actions.

At this point, it's important to note there is no consensus in historic Christianity regarding punishment for sin in hell. While all sin leads to hell, it may not lead to the same punishment in hell. While not explicit—and this is what leads to disagreements in Christianity— there is indication of levels and degrees of punishment in hell, especially as seen in the teaching of Jesus.

After Jesus called his twelve disciples and authorized them to drive out demons and heal diseases, he sent them into ministry. He instructed, "If anyone will not welcome you or listen to your words, leave that home or town and shake the dust off your feet. Truly I tell you, it will be more bearable for Sodom and Gomorrah on the day of judgment than for that town" (Matt. 10:14–15). Similarly, after Jesus had performed many miracles, he condemned the unrepentant towns of Chorazin, Bethsaida, and Capernaum, declaring the city of Sodom to be in a better position on judgment day than they. If Sodom had been given the same opportunities as these cities, it would have remained (11:23–24).

Jesus told the parable of the servants to describe final judgment: "That servant who knows the master's will and does not get ready or does not do what the master wants will be beaten with many blows. But the one who does not know and does things deserving punishment will be beaten with few blows. From everyone who has been given much, much will be demanded; and from the one who has been entrusted with much, much more will be asked" (Luke 12:47–48).

Later, Jesus pointed to the Jewish religious leaders and condemned them for their hypocrisy: "They like to walk around in flowing robes and love to be greeted with respect in the marketplaces and have the most important seats in the synagogues and the places of honor at banquets. They devour widows' houses and for a show make lengthy prayers. These men will be punished most severely" (20:46–47).

These types of passages and others have led many theologians and Christian traditions to believe in "levels and degrees of hell." Issues like stewardship, motivation, and opportunity will play a part in the condemnation assigned to a person. So while all sin apart from the atoning work of Christ leads to death, there may be levels and degrees of hell.

conclusion

In his discussion of Satan, C. S. Lewis stated that the Enemy will first attempt to convince us he doesn't exist. If he is unable to do so, then he will try to deceive us into believing he is all that exists.[3] We are tempted to go from one extreme to the other. Similarly, our flesh (sinful nature) will try to persuade us that our sin really isn't sin and an offense against God; excuses for our sin are readily available. If our flesh can't deceive us on this account, it will work to convince us that everything we do is sinful and equally sinful in the eyes of God. The reasoning is, "You have your sins, I have my sins; we are equally sinful in God's eyes."

Historically and biblically, the purpose of recognizing levels and degrees of sin is to help Christians avoid mortal sins, those sins so dangerous that if one persists in them one could forfeit one's salvation. The New Testament identifies those types of dangerous sins (1 Cor. 6:9–10; Gal. 5:19–21; 1 John 5:16–17). While the Reformed and Baptist traditions are exceptions, most Christian traditions believe salvation can be forfeited. However, the Reformed and Baptist traditions have recognized that even if Christians cannot lose their salvation, some sins are greater impediments to a relationship with God and relationships with others and are, therefore, worse than others.

If Christ is going to save us from our sin, then he must strategically and significantly address the most significant sins of the flesh. While we can't be redeemed from all sin in the present life, we will continue to deal with sins of infirmity as a result of our fallen natural image. Christ must liberate us from sins of the flesh that are most damaging to our relationship with God and each other.

4

the world

OUR SPIRITUAL PROBLEM IS COMMUNAL

> Do not love the world or anything in the world. If anyone loves
> the world, love for the Father is not in them. For everything in
> the world—the lust of the flesh, the lust of the eyes, and the
> pride of life—comes not from the Father but from the world.
>
> —1 John 2:15–16

> For everyone born of God overcomes the world. This is the victory
> that has overcome the world, even our faith. Who is it that overcomes
> the world? Only the one who believes that Jesus is the Son of God.
>
> —1 John 5:4–5

The flesh is not the only enemy of humanity. The New Testament
identifies another: the world. Unfortunately, because the apostles John
and Paul used the word *world* in a variety of ways, confusion arises
over what they meant. Because *world* refers to the entire created order
(John 1:10; 1 Cor. 7:31), some Christians have fallen into a form of
Gnosticism, seeing the material world as inherently evil and not part
of God's redemptive plan. *World* can also be used to describe humanity
collectively (John 3:19; Rom. 1:8) and has led some believers to
forsake human communities for isolationism and monasticism.

However, when John and Paul warned the church about the
world, what they had in mind was fallen humanity as a collective

whole without God (John 15:18–27; 1 Cor. 1:18–25). The world comprises all human communities and all social institutions compromised by sin, living in open or covert rebellion against the kingdom of God. John described a deeply rooted hostility between the world and Christians (John 15:18). The world hates believers because we have a different nature from that of the world (v. 19). We submit to and obey a different "prince" from the world's ruler (12:31; 14:30; 15:20–21). Furthermore, the world's sin is exposed and judged through Christ (15:22, 24; 16:8–11). However, we Christians are sent into the world, and we overcome the world because we are no longer of the world (17:18).

The apostle Paul reiterated John's teaching. The world is guilty before God because of its sin, stands under God's judgment, and has been condemned by God (Rom. 3:6, 19; 1 Cor. 6:2; 11:32). The Spirit of God and the spirit of this world are in complete opposition to one another (1 Cor. 2:12), and the wisdom of the world does not perceive the wisdom of God (1:20). Although we Christians live in the world and interact with the world, we are to be crucified to the world (Gal. 6:14).

In this chapter, we want to begin exploring the world's threat to God's sanctifying work in salvation. If Christ is to be our Redeemer, he must not only save us from the flesh, but also from the world. We will begin by tracing the biblical narrative describing the original goodness of the world and its descent into rebellion against God. Then, we will explore the way the world works to undermine the reign of God in the Christian life. In chapter 5, we will examine how the church that Jesus came to establish through his ministry is the means by which we live in the world and also overcome the world.

the social nature of humanity:
the political image of God in humanity

As we saw earlier in our discussion of humanity's creation, the divine image is found not just in the individual, but in human community as well. The Trinity is at the heart of a Christian understanding of God. We don't believe God is a solitary self, but a communion of infinite love among three persons: Father, Son, and Holy Spirit. The image of God in humanity, as such, is expressed in human relationships of self-giving love, mirroring what is expressed between Father, Son, and Holy Spirit. We are social creatures. Human personhood is defined and developed within our network of relationships.

The biblical account of creation bears witness to our communal existence and its necessity for human flourishing. Genesis 2 describes the creation of Adam prior to Eve in the garden of Eden. He lived in a perfect relationship with God. He communed with God in a way none of us will experience this side of glory. He also existed in complete harmony with the created order. The garden and animals thrived under Adam's direction.

Surprisingly, there was a problem even before the serpent and sin entered the picture. Adam was lonely. Even though he had a perfect relationship with God, a void existed in his life. Nothing existed in the created order to meet Adam's need. Why? Adam had been created for more than a relationship with God and for more than wise stewardship of the garden and its inhabitants. His purpose was to love God with all his being and to exercise loving care of what God had entrusted to him, but he had been created for more: love of neighbor. He had been made for relationships of love with other human beings. Adam could not find his completion in himself; he found it in the love of God *and neighbor*.

Augustine famously asserted, "Our hearts are restless until they rest in you, O Lord."[1] And Augustine was correct. However, we also see our hearts are restless until they find their end in other human relationships as well. Similarly, the French mathematician and Christian philosopher Blaise Pascal taught, "There is a God-shaped vacuum in the heart of every man which cannot be filled by any created thing, but only by God, the Creator, made known through Jesus."[2] Pascal spoke the truth. Yet there appears to be a space in our lives that God can't fill or satisfy with his presence alone, only with other human beings.

The biblical narrative tells us God caused Adam to fall into a deep sleep. He took a rib from Adam's side from which he formed Eve and then brought her to him. Adam's response to God's action and the presence of Eve was one of satisfaction: "This is now bone of my bones and flesh of my flesh," he said (Gen. 2:23). Now Adam had fulfillment in the love of God and neighbor.

While providing the biblical foundation for marriage, Eve's formation and presentation to Adam points to the social nature of humanity and to the human community as bearers of the *imago dei*. Genesis 1 testifies more clearly to this in its portrayal of humanity's creation. God said, "Let us make mankind in our image, in our likeness. . . . So God created mankind in his own image, in the image of God he created them; male and female he created them" (1:26–27). Here, both Adam and Eve together represented the divine image, not as individuals, but as community. The role of community is emphasized further by the command God immediately gave to them, "Be fruitful and increase in number" (v. 28). Genesis 5 repeats the creation narrative of chapter 1 by connecting humanity's role as image bearers to being made male and female together and not as a solitary human being (5:2–3).

The social nature of humanity is poignantly portrayed in the fictional movie *Cast Away*. Chuck Nolan, a Federal Express efficiency expert, is traveling on a plane that goes down in the South Pacific in a violent storm. As the only survivor, he finds himself stranded on a deserted island. The movie focuses on Nolan's fight for survival as he searches desperately for adequate food, water, and shelter. The real threat for Nolan, though, is the mental and emotional anguish caused by loneliness. With only an imaginary friend fashioned from a volleyball he names Wilson, Nolan battles with the will to live. In utter despair, he comes to the realization that without real human company he will be driven to madness and suicide. His loneliness leads him to risk death and leave the island. Nolan must rejoin human society at all costs. After making a raft, he paddles his way past dangerous reefs into the ocean currents, where he makes his way into a shipping lane and is rescued.

While it might be tempting to imagine as Christians that we would fare better than Chuck Nolan under similar circumstances, most likely we would be driven to the brink of despair as well, even with our relationship with God through Christ. God is not enough for us, because he made us for more than friendship with himself. The story of humanity's creation helps us to see we've been created for more than a relationship with God and the created order. God created us for each other.

Humanity's creation in the political image of God is what enabled Adam and Eve to live in perfect love for each another as directed by the moral and natural image. The political image provided the platform for them to develop as persons in relationship. It mediated their affections and will toward God, other human beings, and the created order. It also enabled them to receive and to be formed and shaped by the will and affections of others. In the garden, humanity lived in mutually beneficial, perfectly ordered relationships of love with God and each other. They mirrored, as such, the community of divine persons in the Trinity.

Because of our highly individualistic Western culture, and the elevation of the human self above all else, it can be difficult to see the central role of community in God's plans. The Scriptures, nevertheless, are clear: corporate humanity was God's ultimate purpose for Adam and Eve in the garden and in creation's final consummation. We were created for human community in the beginning, and we will be united with God as a human community in the end.

This is seen clearly in the book of Revelation, which gives three corporate pictures of humanity's final destiny with God. We find the pictures of (1) the bride of Christ, the church comprised as all the saints (Rev. 19:7–8; 21:9); (2) a holy city, the new Jerusalem, where "God's dwelling place is now among the people, and he will dwell with them . . . and be their God" (21:3); and (3) a "healing of the nations," where the nations will walk by the light shining from the "glory of God" (21:23–26; 22:2). The biblical image of life everlasting focuses on our corporate union with emphasis on humanity as a whole, rather than on us individually.

the origin of the world as described
by the apostles John and Paul

Adam and Eve's sin in the garden had devastating consequences. Not only did it create the problem of the flesh for us, it brought about the challenge of the world. The problem of sin is not just with us as individuals, but with us socially as well. The political image of God, the part of the *imago dei* that connects us in relationships, was extensively marred by our first parents' disobedience.

If Genesis 1–2 paints a beautiful picture of God's creation and the grandeur we have as human beings in it, chapters 3–11 vividly describe the chaos caused by sin. Not only are we alienated from God through sin, as portrayed by Adam and Eve's attempt to hide from God (3:8) and their banishment from the garden (vv. 23–24), but also all our other relationships in creation are affected and quickly descend into misery.

This injurious effect is portrayed first through the curses placed upon Adam and Eve. Because of sin, hostility exists between humanity and the serpent (v. 15), and discord abounds in human relationships with the created order (vv. 17–19), including in Adam and Eve's physical bodies (v. 16). Disruption plagues human relationships (vv. 12, 16). The writer of Genesis traced the "wages of sin" in the major stories of Cain and Abel (4:1–17), Noah and the flood (5:28 — 9:28), and the Tower of Babel (11:1–9).

More specifically, while pointing out individual sin and the problems of the flesh, particular focus is on fallen humanity as community. The bickering between Adam and Eve over whom to blame for sin (3:12–13), Cain's jealousy and murder of his brother Abel (4:5, 8), the malformed community arising from "the sons of God and the daughters of humans" (6:2), and the wickedness of humanity in the days of Noah (v. 5) leads to God's assessment of humanity as a whole. We read: "The LORD saw how great the wickedness of the human race had become on the earth, and that every inclination of the thoughts of the human heart was only evil all the time" (v. 5). God repeated this assessment after the flood (8:21). The climax of Genesis 3–11, the culmination of the downward spiral of sin, is the formation of a human city, the Towel of Babel. The purpose of this city is to "make a name for ourselves" (11:4), which is a human social attempt to usurp the centrality of God in the created order.

While God did not allow the construction of this city to be finished (vv. 6–9), fallen humanity has been trying ever since to complete what began at Babel. The Old and New Testaments pick up humanity in revolt against God in the imagery of a city or nation. Ezekiel spoke of an apocalyptic leader, Gog, from the land of Magog, and his allied nations who are archetypal enemies of God seeking to destroy God and the friends of God (Ezek. 38–39). The Gospels speak of the kingdom made up of the children of humanity who in the end will have no place in God's coming reign (Matt. 8:12). They also mention the kingdom of Satan set in opposition to Christ and his kingdom (Matt. 12:26; Luke 11:18); and John addressed the quintessential human city, Babylon, in his apocalyptic vision. Here, Babylon represents every type of human evil and contrasts sharply with the city of God, the New Jerusalem (Rev. 17–18).

Augustine picks up this biblical imagery in his theological masterpiece *The City of God*.[3] He described the world as the "city of man," "the earthly city," "the city of the Devil," and "Babylon." He taught that both the city of God and the city of man are driven by and defined by love. The city of God is driven by the "love of God to the contempt of oneself," whereas the city of man is propelled by "the love of oneself to the contempt of God."

As a community, Augustine argued, fallen human beings place trust in themselves rather than God. The struggle for total independence and self-sufficiency characterizes them. They refuse to submit to the Word of God. Their physical appetites, rather than reason, rule them. Even though they have reason, it is not subject to God's rule. Their thoughts, actions, and desires are disordered: sex for personal gratification, lust for power, implacable hatred of others, vengeful cruelty, and every kind of vice defines human existence.

While Augustine described well the pride and egoism of the city of man as "the love of self," he failed to capture the vain attempts to find ultimate purpose in the love of others, but not ultimately in God and his kingdom. The world is capable of being altruistic, thinking beyond itself, and it has the ability to focus on people and objects outside of itself, but its love for others or for material possessions is disordered.

For example, we see many women who sacrifice themselves on behalf of others, even submitting themselves to physical and emotional abuse. Selfishness is not what defines them. Other people form the center of their lives, and they are willing to do whatever is necessary to see the ones they love succeed. If necessary, they are willing to violate the law of God. They are willing to pay the price. Here we might expand upon Augustine and see the world as oriented and focused on creation, whether on self or other realities instead of on God.

the message of the world

Sin is a distortion of God's creation. We have been created for community, first with God and then with each other. The world is the perversion of human social relationships that brings a false alternative.

Whereas God's original creation of human community immersed us in the life of God and oriented us to God and each other, sin disoriented us. It brought a communal life without God or in rebellion against God. This is the world described by the apostles John and Paul.

A classic story is repeated in church history. A group of pilgrims lives in an unfamiliar kingdom. While they can appreciate what it has to offer, they can never be happy there. They will be miserable until they return home. So they set off on their long and arduous journey. To arrive safely they must make use of the resources around them. They must use some type of transportation by land or water; secure the physical necessities of food, drink, and shelter; and navigate the social customs and expectations of the local citizens to make use of their expertise of the land.

On their trip, however, they get sidetracked. The beauty of the country through which they pass, the pleasure of the food, and the charm of the people beguile them, and they lose sight of their ultimate destination—home. Such is our human condition in life.

Because of sin, we find ourselves far from God. If we're to return to our Father's home, the created order in which we live must not become the ultimate object of our desire and love. It must not distract us from our ultimate end, rather it must only be used to bring us to our ultimate goal—the life everlasting.

Everything God has created is good and a means to an end, which is love and fellowship with him. However, if anything in the created order becomes an end in itself and not a means to the end, it's a diversion. Biblically and theologically, the world seeks to entice us from our true purpose and take what has been created as a means to an end and make it the goal itself.

let specific groups and
social identities define who we are

The world seeks to undermine our journey by centering us on this created order as our end in four primary, but not exhaustive, ways. First, it seeks to define us ultimately by our human social bonds. Families, ethnic groups, classes, genders, sexual orientations, and nationalities become our focus and have the "last word" regarding our identity.

Each of us is born into a particular community, and we participate in the social structures of life. We are wives and husbands, daughters and sons, farmers and teachers, rich and poor, one ethnicity or another, and citizens of a certain nation. The Lutheran tradition names these the "orders of creation" and recognizes them as a gift from God to human existence. Through them we are bound to each other, provide mutual service through our unique gifts and skills to one another, and learn the moral law of God in some sense.

Because of sin, however, our social identities become distorted. Without the lordship of Jesus Christ they become disordered and seek to define our identity above all else. Instead of our identity as God's children and citizens of God's kingdom defining us, the world plots to make our family, tribe, ethnicity, and nationality tell us who we are. We allow the values and ethics of our nationality, our race, and our class to usurp what it is to be a member of the family of God.

How many times in human history have we warred with other Christians, sisters and brothers in Christ, because of our differences in race, nationality, or social class? Church history is filled with accounts of how the world has infected and divided the church, at times co-opting Christianity with its idolatrous agenda.

The French movie *Joyeux Noel* illustrates powerfully the world's attempt to make human national and ethnic identities supreme over Christian unity in Christ. Based on actual events in the trenches of World War 1, a number of allied British and French forces call an impromptu truce with their German enemies on Christian Eve in 1914. The inspiration: the spontaneous singing of the familiar Christmas song "Silent Night" by all three nationalities from their respective trenches. A truce and a service of Christian worship led by a Scottish priest soon followed.

Christmas Day was spent sharing food, Christmas gifts, and fellowship with each other. Their national identities and agendas, their hatred for each other, were overcome by their solidarity in Christ. When they tried to fight as enemies after their brief holiday, the British, French, and German soldiers found they couldn't fight one another. Eventually, the officers and troops from each group had to be replaced.

These men experienced in the celebration of Christmas a communion in Christ with each other that transcended their national and ethnic divisions. They didn't cease being British, French, and Germans, but their social identities came under the lordship of Christ. As such, they overcame the world.

think only of ourselves and look out for number one

Second, the world can consume us with the other extreme as well: self-centered individualism. The Scriptures recognize the sacred worth of each human being as created in the image of God, and places personal responsibility upon the individual for thoughts, words, and deeds in the present life and in the life to come. The Enlightenment's focus on the individual paved the way for human rights in the constitutions of most Western nations, leading to slavery's abolition, free public education, prison reform, women's suffrage, the protection of workers from unscrupulous employers, and countless other human achievements.

The world, however, as affected by sin, seeks to isolate us individually and elevate us to the detriment of the larger community. The goal of hyper-individualism is to liberate us from any restriction or tradition that would place us in responsible covenant relationships with other human beings. Subjective self-expression is the highest good, regardless of the cost to others. Attention is placed on the self-sufficiency of the individual with complete sovereignty over personal human life.

The world deludes us into believing the individual person alone has the moral competence to determine what is right and wrong and the ability to know and understand the truth. The individual becomes the sole judge of what is moral and true. Presently, we are reaping the devastating consequences of "money-grubbing, lust-enslaved, porn-infested, abortive self-indulgence."[4] Our entertainment industry vividly illustrates our present state with its fixation on sex, violence, and flamboyant self-expression. Its interpersonal fruits are loneliness, divorce, and substitution of true human intimacy for sexual experimentation.

One way in which the world's preoccupation with personal independence infects contemporary Christianity is in our hyper-individualized relationships with God. Emphasis is placed so much on a personal relationship with Jesus Christ, a Jesus-and-me mentality, that Christian community, the local church, is neglected. Christians are increasingly seeking to go it alone, saying, in effect, "I need Jesus, but not the church."

Scripture furthermore becomes a love letter from God written directly to individuals. The Christian community is wholly unnecessary in understanding and applying it to life. Even though the Bible was principally written for the church, meant to be read and interpreted in community, we think we all have the individual competence to correctly interpret the Scriptures. We think, "I alone can determine what Scripture means for me."

focus on the physical world and all it has to offer

Third, the world fixes our attention on the created order itself, deceiving us into believing the material universe is all that exists. Reality is only what can be known by our five senses; there is nothing beyond what can be seen, touched, heard, smelled, and tasted. While the physical world is good and we have been appointed by God as full participants in it and entrusted by God as stewards of it, we are tempted to find our ultimate meaning and satisfaction in it.

In our fallen condition, the world leads us headlong into the unbridled pursuit of money and material possessions. It seeks to feed our insatiable physical appetites with its many pleasures. It deceives us into believing we are the masters of the natural order, free to plunder and consume the environment of its resources with little regard of the consequences. And it fosters skepticism and cynicism toward any belief in a reality beyond itself. Materialism, consumerism, hedonism, and atheism are what the world uses to ensnare us.

While there are many examples of how the world's fixation on the physical order has infiltrated the church, from proliferation of the "prosperity gospel" to the loss of world-denying practices like fasting and temperance, our obsession with sex perhaps is most illustrative. Either explicitly or subtly, the world's teaching on sex has infiltrated much of the church. We are led to believe that to be fully human and truly live we must have a robust sex life.

Throughout Christian history, men and women who never married and led lives of chastity in obedience to God were admired and respected, often held up as role models for other believers. In contrast today, if Christians never marry and live celibate lives, they are pitied and looked upon as unfulfilled human beings. For too many Christians, the idea of going their entire lives without sex is seen as a nightmare and unimaginable. Celibacy as a beautiful calling and gifting of the Holy Spirit has largely been forgotten in the church (1 Cor. 7:7).

The sex-saturated culture of the world has led to rampant promiscuity in- and outside Christian marriage. Pornography abounds. While the church continues to decry sexual sin in some pockets, increasingly, modification of traditional Christian sexual norms is found: serial monogamy, cohabitation, sexual experimentation, and so forth. Even when we recognize the truth of historic Christian teaching on the subject, the world gives us ample excuses to abandon it. Its message of physical sexual gratification as a human right and necessity permeates evangelical culture in subtle and overt ways.

leave the physical world behind and focus only on the spiritual

Finally, the world can lead us to the other extreme: Gnosticism. If the world can't deceive us into believing the material world is all there is, then it will try to convince us it is evil. The Gnostics plagued the early church. They believed our physical world, including the human body, is destined for destruction in the life to come. Only the spiritual will exist in heaven, they taught. They thought material existence to be intrinsically evil at worst, and at best a divine mistake. Gnostic salvation, therefore, focused on our liberation from the body and on a birth into a purely spiritual world.

While the physical world is fallen, corrupted, and broken by sin, it's still good. Unfortunately, Gnostic-type thinking has led to the neglect of every part of the physical world and has led people to ignore the plight of the hungry, naked, and oppressed in society. If the physical doesn't matter, then why be concerned with it?

Evidence of Gnosticism abounds in the church. Unfortunately, in many Christian funeral services, unless historical liturgies are used, there's often little or no reference to the departed believer's resurrection at Christ's second coming. Instead, focus is on immediate entrance into heaven and the instant experience of final reward. In ignorance, the disembodied, spiritual existence of a person in death is elevated to the place of ultimate salvation. However, while we may be ushered into God's presence when we die, we are still in the state of death, where the Enemy has the last word over our lives. From a biblical and theological perspective, there is no complete work of redemption without bodily resurrection. To be fully human in the life everlasting means we must have a physical body.

Gnosticism infiltrates our views of the created order as well. As with our physical bodies, many do not see the created order as a part of the life everlasting. While they affirm God's declaration of creation's goodness in Genesis and may recognize the impact of human sin on it, they fail to see the full implications of God's salvation. They say, "It's all going to burn in the end."

Christ came to redeem not only humanity from sin, but all of creation as well. Through Christ's ministry, we will realize the ultimate purposes of God, along with the created order. Creation fully participates with us in God's salvation, now and in the future. The present state of the material world matters to God and should impact how we take care of it today.

conclusion

The world is our enemy as Christians. It is fallen humanity as a collective whole without God, made up of every human community and social institution compromised by sin, living in open rebellion against the kingdom of God.

The world seeks to subvert Christ's full work of redemption in our lives through its lies and distorted truths. It tries to get us to believe and follow one polarity or the other: from too much group identification on one hand, to extreme individualism on the other; and from too much focus on the material world in one instance, to its complete neglect on another. In one way or another, the world focuses our attention on creation, whether on ourselves or other created realities instead of orienting us in the love of God above all else and then the love of neighbor.

In the next chapter, we will discuss different Christian responses to the challenge of the world. How can we be in the world, but not of the world? Then we will explore the role of the church in Christ's work of sanctifying us from the world.

5

the world's solution is the church

Therefore, I urge you, brothers and sisters, in view of God's mercy,
to offer your bodies as a living sacrifice, holy and pleasing to God—
this is your true and proper worship. Do not conform to the pattern
of this world, but be transformed by the renewing of your mind.
—Romans 12:1–2

If you belonged to the world, it would love you as its own.
As it is, you do not belong to the world, but I have chosen you
out of the world. That is why the world hates you.
—John 15:19

As human beings created in the image of God, we're made for community. The biblical account of our beginning in Genesis and of our ending in Revelation bears witness to the truth. The world is our human community broken and distorted by sin. Instead of living in the love of God and neighbor as full citizens of the kingdom of God, we live in rebellion, focused on the creation rather than the Creator. Through misleading messages and half-truths, the world deceives and leads us away from our true purpose in life.

God, however, did not leave us in corruption, but redeems a new human community from the world. He gave Adam and Eve a promise after the fall, what is commonly called the "proto-evangel" (the first good news). It promised that an offspring of Eve would crush the head of the Serpent (Gen. 3:15). What the Enemy of God and of humanity did in the garden, God will overcome.

God began to fulfill his promise by establishing a covenant with Abraham: "I will make you into a great nation . . . and all peoples on earth will be blessed through you" (Gen. 12:2–3). From Abraham a new community, Israel, arose from the desolation left by the world. As a covenant community, the people of Israel were called to be a holy nation and to be separate from the world (Lev. 26:12; Isa. 52:11; Jer. 32:38). God gave them a moral law, reflecting his character (Ex. 19—Num. 10) to help them live as his people in the world.

Through Israel and the birth of Jesus Christ by the Virgin Mary, the eternal Son of God assumed full human nature and became incarnate. God's promise to our first parents and to Abraham culminated in Christ. In his life, death, resurrection, and exaltation, Christ made possible humanity's salvation—not just individually, but corporately as well.

Jesus brought into existence a new community from out of the world. Building upon the foundation of Israel, he incorporated the Gentiles into God's covenant. Just as circumcision was the rite of initiation into the Old Testament community and Passover celebration a sacramental participation in Israel's deliverance from Egypt, so baptism became the initiatory event into the New Testament church and Holy Communion a sharing in Christ's victory on the cross. Through the Holy Spirit, the church is empowered to be holy as God is holy (1 Pet. 1:19). Christ established the ultimate redeemed community, where the values and ethics of the kingdom of God are instilled. The church is the communal heir to final consummation with God. It is the bride of Christ.

the church as the city of God

The church is God's redemption of the world. It's the new humanity created in the image of Christ Jesus. We are saved from the world to live in the community God intended from the foundation of creation. To use the earlier language of Augustine, we are the city of God formed from the city of man. Few passages in the New Testament capture this idea more succinctly and fully than the apostle Paul's letter to the Ephesians.

Ephesians is unique among the Pauline letters. The apostle wasn't responding to any pastoral problem or addressing a personal concern. He had no other purpose for writing than to edify and encourage believers. He wrote it intentionally as a letter to be circulated among the churches. Ephesians therefore provides a window into one of the driving passions in Paul's theology and life. A cursory examination of the letter quickly reveals the church as a central concern in the apostle's thought and in his understanding of the larger purposes of God for humanity.

The overarching theme of Ephesians is the mystery made known in the gospel (1:9; 3:3–6, 9; 5:32; 6:19), revealing that the dividing wall of hostility between Jews and Gentiles had been broken down through Christ's death and resurrection, bringing them together into one body, the church. We are made into one human community, experiencing the promises of God in Christ Jesus (2:11–22; 3:3–6): being reconciled with God and each other.

Paul saw the church, moreover, as the instrument through which this redeemed human community is birthed into existence. The church is the context in which the union (or reunion) of humanity takes place and humanity's relationship with God is restored, forming one holy temple (2:6, 11–18; 3:9–10). As a community where human divisions are overcome in reconciliation, love, and unity, the church exists as a witness in heaven and on earth. It declares "the manifold wisdom of God" to the authorities, rulers, and powers in the heavenly realms that seek to divide humanity (2:11–21; 3:6, 10). The church, as the city of God, sits in glaring contrast to the city of man, and through its unity gives witness to the truth of Christ.

Paul referred to the church in Ephesians as the body of Christ, with Jesus Christ as the head of the body. In previous Epistles, particularly in Romans and 1 Corinthians, Paul used the body metaphor to describe the local church (or a fellowship of house churches), with the head being simply another member of the total body. In Ephesians, however, the body refers to the universal church with Christ as its head. The new humanity brought together in the collective church is inextricably bound together in solidarity, ruled by Christ, and filled with his presence (1:22–23). We are a community under God's sovereignty with his values and ethics governing our lives. This is in stark contrast to the city of man, an idolatrous church made only of human hands.

According to Paul, the union existing among Christians, the unity manifested in the church, reflects and testifies to the oneness of God, from whom all the families of the earth are named (3:14–15; 4:1–6). God's glory is manifested both in Christ Jesus and in the unity of the church (3:21). If the church is not unified, God's work of bringing together all things on earth in Christ will remain incomplete and his plan to unite all creation in Christ will go without witness to the hostile heavenly powers of the world.

Through his life and ministry, Christ overcame the world, and through the Holy Spirit, he brings into existence a community that overcomes the world as well. The church is God's physical instrument by which he brings people out of the city of man and makes them citizens of the city of God.

what exactly is the church?

At this point, we need to pause and ask a critical question: What exactly is the church? At first it seems to be an easy question to answer. But confusion abounds in contemporary Christianity.

If we examine different historic statements on the church based on Protestant, Roman Catholic, and Eastern Orthodox interpretations of Scripture, common themes arise, helping us understand what the church is and how it can be identified. Briefly defined, the church is (1) the body of Christ—the community of followers of Jesus Christ, which is the goal and end of creation—concretely expressed in local churches; (2) the instrument through which God's saving, sustaining, and sanctifying grace is made available to the world; and (3) is identified by the preaching of the pure Word of God, the due administration of the sacraments, and the community rightly ordered.

First, while the church is described in different ways biblically and theologically ("the people of God," "the temple of the Holy Spirit," etc.), the foremost description is "the body of Christ." On a basic level, this body is comprised of all Christians scattered across the earth.

If we ended our description here, however, we might think a Christian is a member of Christ's body without participating in a local church. While extenuating circumstances and exceptions exist, such as a Christian isolated in prison or a believer living where no other Christians exist, there is strong historical consensus that a person isn't a member of the larger body of Christ without being a part of an actual community of believers. The universal church and the local church are inextricably connected.

More precisely, the body of Christ is composed of specific congregations scattered throughout the world. To be a Christian means you are committed to Jesus Christ in a local church. Through the local church, we're joined to the universal body connected to the head, Christ.

The second part of our definition develops more fully the implications of the church as Christ's body. During Jesus' earthly ministry, he was the primary means of God's grace in the world. While God's grace was truly at work elsewhere in the world during his earthly life, God was primarily working through the incarnate Son of God. Through his obedient life, sacrificial death, triumphal resurrection, and exaltation in ascension, Christ objectively accomplished salvation's work, making God's saving, sustaining, and sanctifying grace available to the world.

Similarly, the church manifested in local congregations is now the body of Christ through which God primarily works in the world. The church is the instrument through which the Holy Spirit applies Christ's redemption to human lives individually and corporately. Make no mistake, the church is not the source of God's grace; rather it's the primary means of God's grace.

Finally, the last section addresses the basic identifying marks of the church—the preaching of the pure Word of God, the due administration of the sacraments, and the community rightly ordered. They are, however, more than simple marks by which true churches and denominations can be identified. They are the primary ways through which Christ imparts his grace to us.

Through communication of sound Christian doctrine rooted in the teaching of Scripture, faithful participation in baptism and Holy Communion, and the exercise of redemptive discipline in local congregations, the Holy Spirit forms Christians into the city of God. We can't become the people of God in isolation from these means of grace in Christian community.

the church's strategies against the world

The world as a corrupted, distorted city can be overcome only through the redeemed and restored city—the church. As we saw in the last chapter, the city of man seeks to subvert the city of God with distorted messages and corrupted truths.

The church historically has answered the challenges posed by the world in a number of ways. Perhaps the most famous summary and critique of these responses is H. Richard Niebuhr's *Christ and Culture*.[1] Most descriptions of how the church has tried to be in the world, but not of the world are inspired by Niebuhr's classic work. Using his framework, the church's engagement with the city of man can be divided into four categories from the most thorough rejection of the world to the most positive embrace of it. The categories are: (1) the church against the world; (2) the church and world in tension; (3) the church transforming the world; and (4) the church above the world.

the church against the world

The most pessimistic approach to the world is the church-against-the-world strategy. In this approach, the values and ethics of the kingdom of God as exemplified and taught by Christ are wholly in conflict with the culture of the world. The city of man is totally corrupt, and we must do all we can to remain untainted by it. As such, Tertullian, an early church father from the late second and early third centuries, exhorted Christians to refrain from politics, participation in the arts and theater, and any form of military service.[2]

This strategy also claims that though we can be redeemed as individuals, human institutions, human cultures, and human wisdom are thoroughly evil and must be renounced. Salvation is a call for us to come out of the world and be a separate community. The world is the domain of Satan and doesn't belong to God in any way. If we follow Christ, we must reject any affinity for the city of man and cleave to the city of God. Only then can we grow in the image and likeness of Christ as the church. Focus is placed on rejecting the present world in anticipation of the kingdom to come in the next life. We live as sojourners in enemy territory.

In the early centuries of the church, followers of Jesus were not considered Jews or Gentiles, but a third race. Traditional social identifiers didn't apply to them. The church is a distinct society with its own law and system of ethics. As members of the church, our identity is not linked ultimately to any particular family, nationality, race, or culture. The only defining moniker is "Christian."

In this approach we become salt, light, and leaven in the world by embodying unapologetically as a church the teachings of Christ regardless of our social circumstances and geographical locale. Unbelievers are called to abandon the city of man and join the city of God through repentance and faith in Jesus Christ. There is no straddling the fence. It's either the church or the world.

the church and world in tension

Still pessimistic, but not rejecting entirely the world is the church-and-world-in-tension approach. Martin Luther captured this mentality with his doctrine of two kingdoms. He believed sin is universal and remains throughout earthly life, making it impossible for a truly holy society to be established on earth. God therefore creates one kingdom, comprised of laws, social structures, and human institutions to stem the tide of sin and chaos. At the same time, he makes another kingdom with citizens made up of sinners justified by God's grace through faith in Christ, living out the distinct teachings of Christ as best they can. Christians are firmly rooted in both kingdoms, trying to honor and work within the institutions God has ordained in the world (such as families, governmental authorities, and economic systems) and living out the values of Christ's kingdom. As Christians we live simultaneously in the city of God and the city of man.

As we would expect, however, the two kingdoms are often in conflict, with ethics and methods foreign to one another. As Christians we must tread a crooked and unclear path between the two. We must navigate between competing and conflicting values.

For example, as Christians we're called to turn the other cheek, yet as citizens of a geopolitical country we're commanded to take up arms and fight in wars. As Christians we're taught to spend our money in godly ways, yet as citizens of a nation we must pay taxes, knowing full well our money will be spent in sinful ways. As Christians we're told to forsake wife and children, yet in many societies we are instructed to honor and protect them above all else. Tensions abound![3]

Complicating matters further is the power of sin, pervading both kingdoms and compromising our Christian judgment. God's will in the world is not always clear. As such, Christians who hold to a church and world in tension are "never free of suspicion, yet never lacking hope; suspicion that apparently good things are compromised by sin and hope that God nonetheless is working out his good pleasure through all of the means—worldly and churchly—that he has been pleased to ordain and sustain."[4] So as the church we participate in the world with a deep sense of humility, aware of our blurred vision clouded by sin.

the church transforming the world

The third approach by the church, and more optimistic, is the church transforming the world. Although we Christians see the world as sinful with Christ standing in judgment over it, rather than shun the world or walk with suspicion in the world, we move forward confident in God's power to change the world. Every level of human society—business, entertainment, the arts, the professions, families, education, and government—is capable of being redeemed and transformed into what God intended.

As the city of God, we march boldly into the city of man by God's grace, and we vanquish it. The church, therefore, seeks to shape the world by getting involved with all levels of society and exerting strategic influence and power. The values and ethics of Christ's kingdom drive our agenda as we work by God's grace to make the world approximate in fuller ways the will of God on earth as it is in heaven.

The fundamental cause for the church's optimism is confident belief in Christ's redemptive work for the entire world. While we recognize the world will not be completely transformed before Christ's second coming, significant progress will be made. God's grace made possible through Christ's life, death, and resurrection, and the outpouring of the Holy Spirit will change the world. The gates of hell will not withstand the church's assault.

Another reason for hopefulness is the fact that the church recognizes the world is not thoroughly corrupted. We know the world was created good by God and originally was the city of God. Although sin has corrupted the world, its goodness isn't annihilated, and it can be restored by God's grace. Through common grace given to every person and already at work in the city of man, plus sanctifying grace made available through the city of God, the world can be redeemed. The city of God is committed to the salvation of the city of man, and engages it at every level.

the church above the world

The final and most optimistic approach to the world is the church above the world. Christians who hold this perspective don't believe there is great conflict between the church and the world. The city of God and the city of man are on friendlier terms. All human cultures, societies, and institutions are gifts from God. To be fully realized as a gift, however, they require Christian revelation and the mediation of the church. The good in the world is supplemented and fulfilled by grace, both coming from Christ.

There is no conflict, therefore, between the best the world has to offer and Christ. Rather, there is continuity. For example, Christians can receive Plato's philosophical insights joyfully, even as those insights need Christian theology to perfect them. Evangelical missionaries can seek and use expressions of God's prevenient grace in the cultures of non-Christian peoples.

The church is viewed as simultaneously in and beyond the world, leading people to salvation in heaven yet encouraging all that is best in culture. The church promotes both the temporal goals and the eternal goals of humanity. The church is not against culture, but uses the grace of the gospel to bring to the world what the world can't achieve for itself.

However, while seeing continuity, there is a hierarchy of values, seeing the spiritual as taking priority over the secular. The secular can never be complete apart from the gospel. The church works interdependently with other institutions, but each institution maintains a sense of autonomy and independence. There is distinction between the city of God and the city of man, but they work together to bring the one human community to God's ultimate purpose.

challenges faced by the church's different strategies

After reviewing the major ways the church has responded to the world, a natural question arises: Which approach is right? Each has a different set of weaknesses or natural temptations it must navigate between the ever-shifting polarizing messages of the world.

The church-against-the-world tactic is particularly suited to excel in a society completely opposed to the values and ethics of God's kingdom. The city of man is fully in charge. Here, the church doesn't seek power or try to force its will on society; it simply bears witness to the city of God through its life lived as a community under Christ's reign and its humble proclamation of the gospel. It is willing to suffer gladly and die if necessary on behalf of Christ.

The temptation, though, is to withdraw completely from the world and forget Jesus' Great Commission to "go and make disciples of all nations" (Matt. 28:19). We can live too easily in our "Christian ghettos," isolated entirely from the world. We retreat into our little communities and forget God's love for the city of man.

The church-and-world-in-tension model is most effective when God-ordained institutions in the fallen order are successful. When families, governments, and economies mitigate the power of sin in society, the church then can seek to discern how best to cooperate with these structures to improve humanity's plight, while recognizing they can never fully embody Christian ideals. It thrives in the unresolved tension between our now-and-not-yet present order and the full realization of God's kingdom at Christ's second coming. The temptation, however, is to separate the two spheres completely. Christianity becomes a personal matter, not public. What we believe as Christians doesn't impact the public policy we forge in society.

The church-transforming-the-world paradigm shines when society naturally embraces Christian values or encourages believers to exert their values in human culture. The church uses power to insert its agenda into larger society through government, media, education, and business to help the world approximate in greater ways God's kingdom. Society becomes the extension of the church. The city of man increasingly looks like the city of God.

The temptation here is unbridled greed for power and the costs associated with its pursuit. Lord Acton's caution—"Power corrupts, and absolute power corrupts absolutely"—is appropriate.[5] We risk selling our souls to gain positions of influence, and once in power, unholiness

we are apt to force unwilling people to comply with our agenda. The church turns larger society into a theocracy.

If the church-and-world-in-tension model accentuates the negative—both church and world have been corrupted by sin—the final view of the church above the world highlights the positive: There is good in the world, and the church must embrace it. This perspective empowers the church to embrace the best of human civilizations and seeks to bring them to full expression. More specifically, it has led to the cultivation of indigenous expressions of Christianity unique to particular cultures, such as hip-hop, cowboy, liturgical, and charismatic forms of Christian worship representing the innumerable expressions of the church.

The temptation for the church here is to uncritically baptize cultural values as Christian. The ways of the world can become the ways of the church. It can lose sight of the fact that even the best the world has to offer is corrupted by sin to some extent. The city of God cannot appropriate all the city of man offers.

In each response the church takes to the different manifestations of the world, it must face inherent weaknesses. No strategy frees the church automatically from the threats posed by the world's lies and enticements. Ultimately, no one approach is appropriate to every human culture. Why? Because the world is not monolithic; it changes and adjusts in its rebellion and opposition to the city of God.

Whatever particular agenda the world brings to the fore often dictates the church's response. The world offers many different messages, and often they are not in agreement with each other. The goal is confusion, chaos, and the subversion of Christ's redemptive work in creation. The church's engagement with the world must be

98

responsive to the society around it. The values of God's kingdom don't change, but how they are concretely lived out may.

God's presence in the church overcomes the temptations posed by the world

In any study of the Christian doctrine of God, the attributes of God are always discussed. One of the best-known divine attributes is omnipresence: God's presence fills all time and space and transcends them. We believe God is fully present in every moment and in every place of creation.

While God is omnipresent, he doesn't exist in all time and space in the same way. There are occasions when God is present in different ways. We see this in the Old Testament when Moses met God at Mount Sinai. God was present in that time and place in a way unlike anywhere else in the world. As a consequence, the Israelites stood on holy ground and God commanded them to act accordingly. While God is everywhere in the created order, his presence at Mount Sinai was different.

Likewise, in the New Testament, we see similar occurrences. At Pentecost God manifested himself in the upper room—a particular place—in a way unique until that moment in human history. When Paul encountered Christ on the road to Damascus, God's presence was there in a way Paul had never experienced. He had a divine appointment and reckoning with God. His response was to fall immediately to the ground in humility.

Our Christian understanding of divine omnipresence is what helps us make sense of Jesus' promise to the church: "For where two or three gather in my name, there am I with them" (Matt. 18:20). Christ is present everywhere in his divine nature, but when the church lives and gathers as a community, he exists among us in a way wholly unlike anywhere else.

This is fundamental to the distinction we make between the secular and the sacred. We recognize God is present in both spheres and exercises sovereignty. What distinguishes the two is how he is present. God chooses to hallow certain places and times with his glorified presence. Therefore, while continuity exists between the secular and sacred, a distinction is required. They are treated differently. We don't respond to the secular in the same way we do the sacred. Just as Moses, the children of Israel, and Paul recognized they were on holy ground and acted accordingly, so do we in the glorified presence of God.

More specifically regarding the church, we recognize God is present in and through the church in a way fundamentally different than he is elsewhere in the world. While God is present even in the city of man, his hallowed glory is manifested in the city of God. While he works in the fallen world, it doesn't compare with what he does in the church.

Wherever the church exists, therefore, is the primary means by which God works to redeem the world. In and through the church, the Holy Spirit makes possible the redemption of humanity in Christ Jesus. God saves, sustains, and sanctifies human beings as they hear the Scriptures read and the Word of God proclaimed in community, as they participate in the sacraments of the church, and as they submit to the discipline, order, and life of the local church.

renewal in the *imago dei* as defense against the world

This grace-giving presence of God in the church enables the Christian community to overcome the world. Here Christians experience a progressive renewal in the image and likeness of God, enabling us individually and corporately to recognize the schemes of the city of man and be victorious over them.

While the moral *imago dei* was destroyed in the fall, it is significantly restored through new birth and can be completely rehabilitated in the present life through progressive and entire sanctification. The restored moral image enables holy love to inform our knowledge, decisions, and actions.

While full restoration of the moral image can take place in our lives, the natural and political images remain marred. However, as growth in wisdom, knowledge, understanding, and practice takes place through immersion in the life of the church, we experience renewal in the natural and political images as well.

Through the church's communal reading of Scripture, proclamation of the gospel, instruction in Christian doctrine, practice of the sacraments, and exercise of discipline, our minds begin to be transformed. The stories, philosophies, teachings, and practices that formed us into the city of man begin to recede, usurped by the Christian narrative told by the city of God. We transition from thinking as the world thinks to having the mind of Christ take hold of our being.

Through shared citizenship in the city of God, we learn to love one another. Restoration of the moral and natural images works out practically through the political. Martin Luther, in his *Larger Catechism*, recognized the real, concrete problems faced in Christian relationships: personal slights, unkind words, acts of injustice, festering wounds, petty jealousies, differences of opinion, and destructive gossip. The temptation we face is to forsake the local church over what we have suffered at the hands of other believers.

However, if we leave the local church, Luther argued, we remove ourselves from the very means God intended to make us holy in relationships. Where else are we going to learn to love our enemy, forgive those who have wronged us, and practice patience with annoying people? The church is the crucible in which the political image of God in us is forged anew through concrete practices of love. We learn to love one another not in theory, but in real life.

In the end, this restoration of the moral, natural, and political images in us through God's transforming grace in the church enables us to recognize the distorted messages and deceptions of the world, and it helps bolster us from giving in to the natural temptations faced in the church's different responses to the world.

conclusion

Only through restoration of the *imago dei* in the church can we as the city of God, navigate the treacherous waters of the world. Such renewal of the moral, natural, and political image of God in us doesn't come by dabbling in the church, but by full participation in the church. In this earthly city of God, we experience the community for which we've been created as far as possible in fallen creation and learn to walk in victory over the world.

6

the Devil
OUR ARCHENEMY

Be alert and of sober mind. Your enemy
the devil prowls around like a roaring lion
looking for someone to devour.

—1 Peter 5:8

During a chapel service at Indiana Wesleyan University, I (Jim) spoke on the topic of enemies to our spiritual walk. My sermon identified three big enemies: the world, the flesh, and Satan.

I received more e-mails and letters from students regarding this message than I had ever received before. In fact, students stopped me in the hallways to talk about what I had shared. Many thanked me for giving a message on a topic they feel is seldom dealt with in many of our churches.

The responses I received revealed something else. There is great confusion about the enemies of our souls, especially about the Devil. He is our archenemy.

from angel of light to prince of darkness

The Devil had a stellar beginning, literally. God created him as Lucifer, meaning "shining one" or "brightness." Isaiah 14:12 identifies Lucifer in his original, created state as "morning star, son of the dawn," and Ezekiel 28:12–15 describes him in that state as "the seal of perfection, full of wisdom and perfect in beauty," adorned with "every precious stone," "anointed as a guardian cherub," and "blameless . . . till wickedness was found in you."

However, other Scriptures portray him in human history as an evil villain. His name—Satan, which appears fifty-two times in the Bible—means hater, enemy, or adversary. The name Devil, *sair* in Hebrew and *diabolos* in Greek, means accuser or slanderer. Revelation 12 calls him "the accuser of our brothers and sisters" (v. 10), but also the "great dragon" and "ancient serpent" (v. 9). *Sair* is an appropriate designation of our ancient Enemy because it means "hairy goat." In the Bible, the goat represents what is low and base. We should not be surprised, therefore, to read that when Jesus described how the King judges the nations, he will separate the sheep (the righteous) from the goats (unrighteous). Matthew 25:33 tells us, "He will put the sheep on his right and the goats on his left." According to verse 41, he will banish those on his left "into the eternal fire prepared for the devil and his angels."

The Devil is also designated "Beelzebul, the prince of demons" (Matt. 12:24). Matthew 13:19 calls him "the evil one," and 2 Corinthians 6:15 calls him "Belial," meaning "worthlessness." Further, Jesus referred to the Devil as "the prince of this world" (John 12:31). In his role as prince of this world, the Devil rules supreme over the evil world system.

So what happened? How did Lucifer, this angel of light that guarded God's throne, become the Prince of Darkness, God's avowed enemy and ours?

evil ambition and swift judgment

Isaiah 14 draws aside the curtain of predawn human history to provide a glimpse of what transpired when Lucifer, the morning star angel, fell from his lofty position at God's throne. Though Isaiah's text is directed to the human king of Babylon, many scholars agree with a long Christian tradition that sees Satan's story mirrored in this human history.

Not content to be near the throne where he could serve and worship God, Lucifer wanted to sit on the throne of the Most High and be worshiped as God. Verses 13–14 relate the story of Lucifer's incredibly wicked ambition: "You said in your heart, 'I will ascend to the heavens; I will raise my throne above the stars of God [angels]; I will sit enthroned on the mount of assembly, on the utmost heights of [the sacred mountains]. I will ascend above the tops of the clouds; I will make myself like the Most High."

Ezekiel 28:11–19 also gives what scholars and tradition have seen to be another metaphorical glimpse of Lucifer's wicked ambition, described through Ezekiel's prophetic message addressed to the prince of Tyre. Addressing Lucifer, verses 17–18 say, "Your heart became proud on account of your beauty, and you corrupted your wisdom because of your splendor. . . . You have desecrated your sanctuaries."

The psalmist said, "Your throne, O God, will last for ever and ever" (Ps. 45:6); and Jeremiah wisely wrote, "You, LORD, reign forever; your throne endures from generation to generation" (Lam. 5:19). Nothing can topple God from his throne. Lucifer should have known this truth, but he was driven by sinful ambition, not truth.

Judgment swiftly befell Lucifer. God cast him out of heaven and down to the earth (Isa. 14:12). He was "brought down to the realm of the dead, to the depths of the pit" (v. 15).

Because of his sin, Lucifer's nature became altogether evil (John 8:44; 1 John 3:8). Sin corrupted his wisdom (Ezek. 28:17). He will eventually be disallowed access to God, where he now accuses believers (Rev. 12:7–10). Jesus judged him at the cross (John 12:31). And ultimately, he will be consigned eternally to the lake of fire (Rev. 20:10).

the Devil tempted the first humans

God created our first parents, Adam and Eve, in his own image (Gen. 1:27). He blessed them and provided everything they needed for a peaceful, happy relationship with him and each other. The garden of Eden, in which he placed them, was perfect. God had made all kinds of trees that were pleasing to the eye and good for food (2:9). Even the animals shared a peaceful relationship with one another (vv. 19–20). The first humans tended the garden in productive, serene conditions (v. 15). Work was void of harshness. They did not have to combat weeds or insects. And God gave them only one prohibition: "You must not eat from the tree of the knowledge of good and evil" (v. 17). The consequence of failing to honor the prohibition was death (v. 17).

The sentence of death would extend to the entire human race and would include more than physical death (Rom. 5:12; Heb. 9:27). It would also include spiritual death and eternal death (Eph. 2:1; Rev. 20:10–15). When someone physically dies, his or her spirit separates from the body. With spiritual death, the unbeliever is separated from God in this life. With eternal death, the unbeliever is separated from God in eternity.

In the beginning, everything was perfect, peaceful, and productive, but something evil changed all that. Satan entered the garden by way of a serpent and successfully tempted Adam and Eve.

In the garden of Eden, Eve saw that the prohibited tree was good for food, pleasant to the eyes, and desired to make one wise. For this reason, she took some of the fruit and ate it, also giving it to Adam who was with her (Gen. 3:6).

Almighty God told Adam and Eve they were not to eat from the Tree of Knowledge of Good and Evil. But the serpent came to them and told them they would be like God if they ate fruit that came from that tree. John White wrote in *The Fight* that the fruit "was good for food (lust of the flesh), and that it was a delight to the eyes (lust of the eyes), that the tree was to be desired to make one wise (the pride of life). In this biblical account the lust of the flesh, the lust of the eyes, and the pride of life all worked in sinister collaboration," leading them to disobey God and causing sin to enter the world.[1]

Genesis 3:1 describes the Devil in the form of the serpent as "more crafty than any of the wild animals the LORD God had made." He employed his craftiness first by placing doubt in Eve's thinking: "Did God really say . . . ?" he asked (v. 1). Undoubtedly, he tries to plant doubt in our minds too when he tempts us to disobey God's Word. "Did God really tell me to be holy?" "Did he really tell me to love my neighbor as myself?" "Did he really say I should not covet?"

Sadly, Eve added to the prohibition God had given her and her husband. She added, "You must not touch it" (v. 3). Adding to God's Word sets us up for failure. We see God as harsh and impossible to please, which is exactly how the Devil wants us to think of him. Finally, the Devil contradicted God's Word. "You will not certainly die," he told Eve (v. 4).

Satan's battle against the Bible is one of the biggest battles he wages today. He persuades some Christians that the Bible is not relevant. He leads them to think it is simply an archaic book that they can ignore. He persuades other Christians that the Bible is not fully inspired and it is their prerogative to decide which parts of it are reliable and which are not. He tries to wear down our confidence in Scripture so we will fall away from our relationship with God's holiness. Those separated from God risk committing sin without feeling guilty or being accountable to God.

If the Devil cannot erode our confidence in God's Word, he can still assault us at our weakest points, and he uses the lust of the flesh, the lust of the eyes, and the pride of life as his assault weapons.

falling to the lust of the flesh, the lust of the eyes, and the pride of life

Scripture presents many examples of those who fell by yielding to the lust of the flesh, the lust of the eyes, and the pride of life. Here are a few from the Old Testament.

After returning home from what must have been a disappointing day of hunting, Esau was famished and smelled stew that his younger twin Jacob was cooking. Foolishly, he traded his birthright to Jacob for some stew. In doing so, he placed a higher value on satisfying his flesh than on retaining his birthright, which included not only a double share of his father's inheritance, but also the blessings and privileges of being the family's spiritual leader (Gen. 25:29–34).

Samson started as a Nazirite, separated unto God (Judg. 13:5). And with enormous strength, he began to deliver Israel from the Philistines. However, his life ended as the Philistines' prisoner. They gouged out his eyes, shackled him, and made him grind wheat in the prison. At a sacrifice to honor their god Dagon, the Philistines drew him into their temple and mocked him. Samson had fallen victim to the lust of the flesh and the lust of the eyes by seeing and marrying a pagan woman, spending the night with a pagan prostitute, and romancing another pagan woman (14:1, 10; 16:1, 4).

When pastureland became too crowded for both Abraham and his nephew Lot's flocks and herds, Abraham gave Lot first choice of additional land. Lot looked and saw how well watered the plain of Jordan was, so he made it his choice (Gen. 13:8–11). It did not seem to matter to him that his choice would put him in close proximity to and association with the wicked people of Sodom. The lust of the eyes eventually resulted in his spiritual decline, the loss of his material possessions, his wife, and his moral integrity (19:15–36).

After entering Canaan, the Israelites enjoyed a miraculous victory over the well-fortified city of Jericho, but soon met defeat at the hands of the defenders of the town of Ai. What had caused this calamity? The blame lay at the feet of Achan. Although he knew the Lord had commanded the Israelites to keep away from the spoils of Jericho because they were to be devoted to the Lord (Josh. 6:18–19), Achan took from Jericho "a beautiful robe . . . two hundred shekels of silver and a bar of gold" and buried them in his tent (7:21). He had succumbed to the lust of the eyes. In his confession to Joshua, Achan said, "When I saw in the plunder . . ." (v. 21).

Even Israel's beloved King David caved to temptation, perhaps falling to all three avenues of temptation. He saw beautiful Bathsheba and desired her (lust of the eyes), committed adultery with her (lust of the flesh), and arranged the murder of her husband (pride of life). He used his authority as king to obtain Bathsheba and have her husband killed in battle (2 Sam. 11).

In the New Testament, we also find examples of those who succumbed to the Devil's prominent avenues of temptation.

The lust of the flesh caused Demas to forsake the apostle Paul. He did so because he loved the world (2 Tim. 4:10). He must have craved a softer life more than that of associating with prisoner Paul.

Judas, who betrayed Jesus, lusted for the betrayal award of thirty pieces of silver. Apparently, his eyes were focused upon what the money might mean to his economic and social status. Satan entered Judas just before he left the Passover Feast with Jesus and the disciples to pursue the betrayal.

When the church was still in her infancy, Ananias and his wife, Sapphira, succumbed to the temptation of pride. They wanted to be honored for giving what they pretended to be the full amount of the sale of a piece of property. However, the Holy Spirit revealed their hypocrisy to Peter, and they both paid for their sin with their lives (Acts 5:1–10).

The avenues of temptation Satan used in the garden of Eden stretched through Bible history and continue today. We must recognize them as threats to holiness and resist them in the power of the Spirit. Galatians 5:16–18 instructs, "Walk by the Spirit, and you will not gratify the desires of the flesh. For the flesh desires what is contrary to the

Spirit, and the Spirit what is contrary to the flesh. They are in conflict with each other, so that you are not to do whatever you want. But if you are led by the Spirit, you are not under the law."

the temptation of Jesus

Immediately after Jesus' baptism, the Spirit led him into the desert to be tempted by the Devil (Matt. 4:1). After fasting forty days and forty nights, Jesus was physically weak and hungry. That's when Satan assaulted him with temptation.

In the wilderness, Satan, the tempter, approached Jesus and said, "If you are the Son of God, tell these stones to become bread" (v. 3). Preachers have identified this temptation as representing the lust of the flesh. Satan then took Jesus to the holy city, had him stand on the highest point of the temple, and said to him, "If you are the Son of God . . . throw yourself down. For it is written: 'He will command his angels concerning you, and they will lift you up in their hands, so that you will not strike your foot against a stone'" (v. 6) — the pride of life. And in verse 8, we are told that Satan took Jesus up "a very high mountain and showed him all the kingdoms of the world and their splendor. 'All this I will give you,' he said, 'if you will bow down and worship me,'" which represents the lust of the eyes.

Theologians have debated for decades, perhaps centuries, whether Jesus could have succumbed to Satan's temptations and sinned. Some insist he could not have yielded to the temptations because he did not have a sin nature, therefore, there was nothing in him to which temptation could appeal. Others argue he could have sinned because he was a real human being. If he could not have sinned, they argue, the temptations were not really temptations.

It is not our intention to enter this debate, but suffice it to say Jesus triumphed over each temptation in the same way we can triumph over temptation. He confronted each temptation by quoting Scripture. "It is written," he said (vv. 4, 7, 10). In our battles with our archenemy we need to use "the sword of the Spirit, which is the word of God" (Eph. 6:17). Just as Jesus employed a specific, applicable Scripture passage to rebuff Satan, so we should know the Bible well enough to apply specific verses to specific temptations. We should strive to be able to say truthfully what the psalmist wrote: "I have hidden your word in my heart that I might not sin against you" (Ps. 119:11).

the Devil attacks our faith

The book of Job alerts us to the fact that Satan appears before God to accuse the faithful and to attack their faith. Job seemed to have lived before any Scripture was written, yet he was "blameless and upright; he feared God and shunned evil" (Job 1:1). He was a family man and a very wealthy rancher. When his sons and daughters feasted in his sons' homes, Job would sacrifice early in the morning, thinking they might have sinned and cursed God in their hearts (vv. 2–5).

Satan took notice of Job's faith and devotion. One day he appeared before the Lord and suggested Job feared God only because God was protecting him, his household, and his possessions, and was prospering him. Satan suggested Job would curse God if God would strike everything that belonged to Job. God responded by giving Satan permission to test Job (vv. 6–12).

Satan rushed to the task at hand. In rapid succession, he used marauders and a lightning-caused fire to wipe out Job's livestock and servants. And then he used a mighty wind to collapse the house in which Job's sons and daughters were feasting. They died under the rubble (vv. 13–19). Upon receiving all this bad news, Job grieved, and then "fell to the ground in worship and said: 'Naked I came from my mother's womb, and naked I will depart. The Lord gave and the Lord has taken away; may the name of the Lord be praised'" (vv. 20–21). Job's faith in God remained firm. He did not sin by blaming God (v. 22).

The next time Satan appeared before God, he told God that Job would curse him if Job's own life was under attack (2:1–5). With utmost confidence in Job, God allowed Satan to attack Job's health short of killing him (v. 6).

Satan "afflicted Job with painful sores from the soles of his feet to the crown of his head" (v. 7). In this affliction, Satan had an assistant, Job's wife. She advised Job to "curse God and die" (v. 9). But Job said to her, "You are talking like a foolish woman. Shall we accept good from God, and not trouble?" (v. 10). Again, "Job did not sin in what he said" (v. 10). His faith in God remained firm.

Job continued to be buffeted by Satan, and although Job did not understand why he was the target of so many trials and the object of accusatory counselors, he patiently trusted in God. Finally, God gave Job a fresh revelation of himself, vindicated Job, doubled his livestock from what it was before the trials, and gave him another seven sons and three daughters.

Genuine faith understands that God is holy and will not allow any trial to enter our lives unless it is for our good and his glory. Indeed, "We know that in all things God works for the good of those who love him, who have been called according to his purpose" (Rom. 8:28).

The apostle Paul, too, suffered a persistent attack from Satan. He called it "a thorn in my flesh, a messenger of Satan, to torment me" (2 Cor. 12:7). He pleaded with the Lord three times to remove the thorn, but God left it in place. Nevertheless, alongside the thorn he placed his grace. God told Paul, "My grace is sufficient for you, for my power is make perfect in weakness" (v. 9).

As long as the Devil prowls around like a roaring lion looking for people to devour (1 Pet. 5:8), we can expect trouble and trials, but God's grace is all-sufficient.

conclusion

Satan is the believer's worst enemy, and he is also the craftiest. He despises God, hates God's redemptive work, and seeks to destroy God's people. But Satan is a defeated foe, and his time is limited. Someday God will cast him into the lake of fire. In the meantime, we must resist him in the faith, stay loyal to God, and persevere in holiness. Regardless of the temptations and harsh trials Satan inflicts on us, "we are more than conquerors through him who loved us" (Rom. 8:37).

the Devil's evil minions

For our struggle is not against flesh and blood, but against the rulers, against the authorities, against the powers of this dark world and against the spiritual forces of evil in the heavenly realms.
—Ephesians 6:12

When Lucifer, the Devil, rebelled against God in pre-human history, he led a host of other angels in his attempt to dethrone God. They suffered the same fate as their traitorous leader: God cast them down. The Bible refers to them as the Devil's angels, evil spirits, and demons. Jude wrote about "angels who did not keep their positions of authority but abandoned their proper dwelling" and that God has kept them bound "with everlasting chains for judgment on the great Day" (Jude 6). Jude 7 compares the sin of those angels with the "sexual immorality and perversion" of Sodom and Gomorrah and the surrounding towns.

worship of false gods

Worship of false gods did not end with the Old Testament. It continues to this present age. Therefore, the apostle John instructed us to "test the spirits to see whether they are from God, because many false prophets have gone out into the world" (1 John 4:1). The apostle Paul warned, "The Spirit clearly says that in later times some will abandon the faith and follow deceiving spirits and things taught by demons" (1 Tim. 4:1). To be sure, demons do not appear as little imps with horns, a tail, and a pitchfork. They lure many people into false religion by appearing as "apostles of Christ" (2 Cor. 11:13). Paul noted, "Satan himself masquerades as an angel of light. It is not surprising, then, if his servants also masquerade as servants of righteousness" (vv. 14–15).

How is it possible that so many churches that once believed the Bible and proclaimed the gospel no longer do so? What turned them from biblical churches to centers of liberal theology? In many cases, a pastor arrived whose personality was so charming and his words so smooth that he caught the congregants off guard. He seemed so nice that hardly anyone questioned what he taught in his sermons. No one seemed to notice how smoothly and suavely he introduced "things taught by demons" (1 Tim. 4:1).

demons are real and vicious enemies

Scripture acknowledges that Satan and his army of demons do exist. Matthew 8:28 reports that two demon-possessed men came out to meet Jesus. Now we must understand the warning that some the Devil's evil minions

give. C. S. Lewis cautioned against imagining a demon behind every tree. But he also warned us about the danger of not believing Satan exists. He wrote, "There are two equal and opposite errors into which our race can fall about the devils. One is to disbelieve in their existence. The other is to believe in them and to feel an excessive and unhealthy interest in them."[1]

We need to take Lewis's words to heart. We must be concerned about those who claim to be believers in Christ but whose lives show they do not believe in the reality of Satan and his army. The Bible is not ambiguous on the reality of Satan and spiritual warfare.

The following are some verses showing that Jesus Christ recognized the existence of Satan and his army:

- Matthew 4:1, 10 says, "Then Jesus was led by the Spirit into the wilderness to be tempted by the devil. . . . Jesus said to him, 'Away from me, Satan!'"
- In Matthew 10:1, "Jesus called his twelve disciples to him and gave them authority to drive out impure spirits and to heal every disease and sickness."
- When Jesus spoke in private to his disciples (Matt. 17:14–20), he rebuked them for their little faith, but did not rebuke them for attempting to cast out demons.
- Matthew 25:41 tells us Jesus said, "Then [God] will say to those on his left, 'Depart from me, you who are cursed, into the eternal fire prepared for the devil and his angels.'"
- Matthew 12:22–28 tells us that Jesus was accused of casting out demons in the name of Beelzebul, the prince of demons. He explained to his critics that he was driving them out by the Spirit of God.

- Matthew 8:16 states, "When evening came, many who were demon-possessed were brought to him, and he drove out the spirits with a word and healed all the sick."
- John 8:44 describes Jesus as talking to people who were not true believers. He said, "You belong to your father, the devil, and you want to carry out your father's desires. He was a murderer from the beginning, not holding to the truth, for there is no truth in him. When he lies, he speaks his native language, for he is a liar and the father of lies."

As the above verses show, Jesus himself spoke about Satan and his demons as being real. In fact, a significant amount of Jesus' time was spent freeing people from them.

The writers of the New Testament Epistles and Revelation also wrote about Satan and his army:

- Paul wrote in 2 Corinthians 11:13–14, "For such people are false apostles, deceitful workers, masquerading as apostles of Christ. And no wonder, for Satan himself masquerades as an angel of light."
- Peter wrote, "Be alert and of sober mind. Your enemy the devil prowls around like a roaring lion looking for someone to devour. Resist him, standing firm in the faith, because you know that the family of believers throughout the world is undergoing the same kind of sufferings" (1 Pet. 5:8–9).
- In Revelation 12:7–9, John wrote, "Then war broke out in heaven. Michael and his angels fought against the dragon, and the dragon and his angels fought back. But he was not strong enough, and they lost their place in heaven. The great dragon

was hurled down—that ancient serpent called the devil, or Satan, who leads the whole world astray. He was hurled to the earth, and his angels with him."

Over one hundred times, the New Testament affirms the reality of Satan and his demons. We see him in the very early chapters of Genesis all throughout the books to Revelation. He is mentioned in seven books of the Old Testament, and nineteen books of the New Testament speak about him, with all of the New Testament writers represented. In Genesis 3:1, we see Satan tempting Eve. In 1 Chronicles 21:1, we see him encouraging King David to take a census that was not God's will for David to do. Revelation 12:9 portrays Satan cast out from heaven along with his fellow rebels. Jesus spoke of Satan no less than twenty-five times. He certainly believed Satan exists.

As with the holy angels, the Bible makes no effort to prove the existence of fallen angels—demons—and Satan. It merely assumes their existence, as it relates various details about him and how he operates. For the believer, shouldn't this be enough evidence? Why? Because nothing is more reliable than the testimony of the Holy Scriptures.

Satan is not omnipresent, omniscient, or omnipotent by any stretch; but his demons are so numerous that they serve his pernicious purposes and comprise a potent force for evil. Paul informed the Ephesians and us that "our struggle is not against flesh and blood, but against the rulers, against the authorities, against the powers of this dark world and against the spiritual forces of evil in the heavenly realms" (Eph. 6:12). He preceded this exhortation by telling us to "stand against the devil's schemes [strategies]" (v. 11).

strategies of the Devil and his evil minions

Knowing that there is an Enemy is not enough. It is also important to know how this Enemy operates. The apostle Paul warned
believers in 2 Corinthians 2:11 to be wary "in order that Satan might
not outwit us. For we are not unaware of his schemes."

Satan deceives and tempts

Satan does not come to us transparently ugly and scary, but
appears as one who is beautiful, handsome, and winsome. People
are attracted to his agenda because he will dress it up and seduce
them with it. W. E. Vine informs us that the word *deceive* means
"giving a false impression." This is exactly what Satan does to trap
and destroy people.[2]

Satan also tempts us. For this reason he is also called the tempter.
He seeks to exploit a person's perfectly good desires and entice that
individual to fulfill them by improper means. That is why all good
gifts that come from above—food, rest, sex, ambition, and work—
have distorted and twisted variations that are far from the will of
God. Satan's big desire is to have Christians fall away spiritually
from God. ElRay Christiansen wrote, "Satan knows all the tricks.
He knows where we are susceptible to temptations and how to entice
us to do evil. He and his messengers suggest evil, minimize the
seriousness of sin, and make evil inviting."[3] This is how Satan operates. Satan lies and deceives people. Jesus described Satan as the
Father of Lies (John 8:44). It has been said that human sin has a
dual source. There is first the human source whereby the individual
makes wrong choices. And there is also the supernatural source, or
Satan's deceptive temptations. He has a way of planting evil

thoughts in people's minds. They sound wonderful at first, but if acted upon, they lead to destruction.

Satan gets people to believe that his counterfeit pleasure is the only way to satisfy their emotional needs. He'll offer sex from a video screen in a perverted way, moving them away from what is good, true, loving, and wonderful, and twisting it into something that is evil and destructive. The counterfeit pleasure will always look and taste attractive. But the problems may not come for weeks, months, or even years.

Satan seeks to murder

Jesus called Satan a murderer (John 8:44). Jesus used this description to convey the message that Satan and his army can resort to violence and can render physical harm and even death.

In Job we are told that Satan used a violent storm to kill Job's ten children. In Mark 5:1–20, we read about a man with an impure spirit living in the tombs of the region of the Gerasenes. He cried out day and night and cut himself with stones. And in Mark 9:22, we have the record of a demon trying to physically destroy a young boy by casting him into fire and water.

The Old Testament relates that after the Lord departed from King Saul an evil spirit (a demon) came upon him (1 Sam. 18:10). Consequently, while David was playing his harp for Saul, Saul hurled his spear at David in an attempt to kill him (v. 11). David escaped, but repeatedly afterward Saul pursued David with the intent to kill him.

Wilbur O'Donovan, a missionary in West and East Africa for over thirty years asks, "One wonders how many crimes of murder, tribal wars, religious wars and national wars have been brought about in history by the suggestions of demons to the minds of men?"[4] Surely, demonic influence lies at the root of many homicides today.

Satan seeks to hinder one's prayer life

When we study Daniel's life of faith in Daniel 9, we discover that he was a man of prayer. He prayed for God's mercy when he realized that his people would be liberated from the captivity of the Babylonian Empire. In Daniel 10, we learn that Daniel prayed and fasted for three weeks. When God saw what his servant was doing, he sent his angel to strengthen Daniel. But according to verse 13, this angel was detained for twenty-one days by the Devil. The angel said to Daniel, "But the prince of the Persian kingdom resisted me twenty-one days. Then Michael, one of the chief princes, came to help me, because I was detained there with the king of Persia."

Satan is diligent in his effort to hinder God's children from establishing a strong and consistent prayer life. We often feel guilty for not spending time in prayer on a daily basis. But we justify it by saying there is so much we need to do.

In his sermon "When Satan Hinders You," Charles Spurgeon preached, "Satan is sure to hinder us when we are earnest in prayer. He checks our importunity, and weakens our faith in order that, if possible, we may miss the blessing. Nor is Satan less vigilant in obstructing Christian effort."[5]

Satan seeks to discourage God's servants

Satan and his forces have a plan to terrorize our souls, to render us impotent as believers, to make us think we are worthless to the cause of Christ, and to make our lives characterized by misery and spiritual defeat. John Wesley, in his sermon "Satan's Devices," wrote, "Satan endeavours to destroy the first work of God in the soul, or at least to hinder its increase, by our expectation of that greater work. . . . He endeavours to damp our joy in the Lord, by the consideration of our own vileness, sinfulness, unworthiness."[6]

I (Jim) was scheduled to preach at chapel a couple days after we had an encouraging and captivating guest speaker. He captured the attention of everyone in the audience. In those two days that passed, I kept hearing an inner voice say to me, "You're not as good as the guest speaker. You will never be as good as he is, so why even try? Instead of students commenting about how good you are, they will be critiquing you to find all the ways you are not a good preacher. They will describe you as a dud."

When I should have been sleeping, I was waking up at 3 a.m. The voice was still speaking words of discouragement to me. "Did you notice that the guest speaker was able to keep everyone's attention? You wouldn't be able do that! People are going to fall asleep while you preach!"

I woke up the morning I was supposed to speak so exhausted that I wanted to run away. As I walked into the chapel auditorium one of my student chaplains saw me and exclaimed, "You look horrible! Didn't you sleep well last night? Are you ready to preach in chapel this morning?"

"To be honest with you, I feel exhausted and, if I had my way, I would run away so someone else, who can do a better job, could speak this morning."

I have discovered through the years that students can share wonderful truth when needed. This young man looked at me and boldly stated, "Dr. Lo, listen to yourself! You are falling prey to Satan's scheme. He wants you to feel down about yourself and give up serving God. You have been appointed to preach in chapel this morning. Depend upon God, and he will be there to help you. But don't allow Satan's schemes to discourage, defeat, and destroy you!"

Satan is able to perform deceiving miracles

As we have noted, demons inspire and promote false religion. Sometimes Satan performs counterfeit miracles to do so. He did so in Egypt, when Moses and Aaron instructed Pharaoh to release the Hebrews from slavery. When Aaron obeyed God's commands, miraculous plagues occurred. But Pharaoh's idolatrous magicians performed copycat miracles by using their secret arts (Ex. 7–8).

In the end times, a false prophet will emerge in Israel and draw worship away from God and direct it to a powerful dictator. The dragon (the Devil) will empower him to perform "great signs, even causing fire to come down from heaven to the earth in full view of the people" (Rev. 13:13). Verse 14 reports that he "deceived the inhabitants of the earth" and "set up an image in honor of the beast who was wounded by the sword and yet lived [the dictator]." Satan will instate both wicked opponents of God in their positions of authority and use both as his spokespeople (vv. 2, 4–5).

We live in a world in which visual images are highly valued. Advertisers know how persuasive visual messages are, but visual messages can deceive us if we are not careful. We must exercise discernment when we observe what seems to be a miracle. It may be a counterfeit miracle demonically induced to draw us away from the true God of might and miracles.

conclusion

Hordes of unholy angels follow the Devil as his willing servants. They are demons, also called evil spirits and fallen angels. Like their master, the Devil, they are incorrigibly wicked, pernicious, and bent on opposing God and his people. They endeavor to make us unholy and useless servants of God. They attack us relentlessly, tempting us, discouraging us, deceiving us, and trying to destroy our prayer life. Nevertheless, as the apostle John pointed out, the "one who is in [us] is greater than the one who is in the world" (1 John 4:4).

As we shall see in the next chapter of this book, God has equipped us to triumph over the Devil and his evil minions.

8
winning the war

Thanks be to God! He gives us the victory
through our Lord Jesus Christ.
— 1 Corinthians 15:57

We should avoid two grave errors in our struggle against Satan.
The first is that of underestimating his power. The second is that of
overestimating our ability to triumph over him in our own strength.
The Devil is a powerful enemy. He is cunning, forceful, and able
to defeat us if we underestimate his power. However, he is not
omnipotent, and God has provided all we need to resist him and lead
a holy life.

instructions to repent and
recover love for God

In the letter from Revelation our risen Lord dictated to the church at Ephesus, he commended the believers for their hard work, perseverance, and loyalty to sound doctrine, but he criticized them for having forsaken their first love (Rev. 2:1–4). He commanded, "Consider how far you have fallen! Repent and do the things you did at first" (v. 5).

Holding sound doctrine and staying busy for the Lord cannot keep us safe from the Devil's attacks. How often have we learned about a well-known pastor's fall into sin, not because he denied sound doctrine or maintained a busy schedule, but because his love for the Lord had grown cold? If he had loved the Lord supremely, he would not have fallen into an illicit love affair. Love for God and love for sin are mutually exclusive.

Of course, declining love for God may not lead to an illicit affair, but it can lead to other sins. It might lead to the love of money, pleasure, prestige, possessions, selfish ambition, or a number of other sins. Keeping our love for the Lord healthy will result in obeying him instead of sinning against him. Jesus said, "If you love me, keep my commands" (John 14:15).

If we examine our hearts and lives and discover our love for the Lord is weaker than our first love, we need to repent and recover our first love. To repent means to change the mind. Although sorrow is not in the word's meaning, it is hard to see how sorrow is not part of true repentance. How can we offend our loving and holy heavenly Father and not feel sorry? When David repented of adultery, he experienced deep sorrow. He had lost his joy and longed to recover it (Ps. 51:8, 12). He realized that God would not despise "a broken and contrite heart" (v. 17).

recognize the Enemy

Paul informed us that our "struggle is not against flesh and blood, but against the rulers, against the authorities, against the powers of this dark world and against the spiritual forces of evil in the heavenly realms" (Eph. 6:12). These identifications likely apply to ranks of evil spirits marshaled under Satan. They are capable of discouraging us, tempting us, distracting us, and even oppressing us unless we oppose them in the strength and power of the Lord (v. 10).

When Jesus told his disciples they would all fall away from him in the hour of his greatest need, Peter replied self-confidently, "Even if all fall away on account of you, I never will" (Matt. 26:33). Soon, when confronted by a young servant girl, Peter learned how weak he was. He denied the Lord three times (vv. 69–75). Satan had wanted to destroy Peter, but Jesus prayed for Peter, and eventually Peter recovered from his denial (Luke 22:31). He later advised us to be alert, because the Devil looks for potential victims (1 Pet. 5:8).

Often, conflict tears a church apart. Members quarrel with each other. Feelings get hurt. Accusations fly. Wounds become deep. But fellow believers are not our enemy. God is the author of love (Rom. 5:5; 1 Cor. 13); he is not the author of confusion (1 Cor. 14:33).

live by the Spirit

The Devil appeals to our sin nature in order to get us to sin, so Paul told the Galatian believers to "walk [or live] by the Spirit, and you will not gratify the desires of the flesh" (Gal. 5:16). Living by the Spirit involves a consistent, moment-by-moment dependence upon the Spirit to help us lead a holy life, to do God's will, and to say no to temptation. A holy life involves a walk, not a single step. So, if we want to defeat the Enemy of our souls, we must follow the Spirit's guidance and draw upon his power (Eph. 5:15–20).

take your stand!

On April 2, 2015, al-Shabaab militants attacked Garissa University College in Kenya and murdered 147 people. During the assault, they hunted down Christians who were praying, and asked whether they were Christians. If a student took a stand for Christ, he or she was gunned down immediately. Christians in North America may never have to face a murderous militant religious enemy, but daily we face Satan, the Enemy that kindles evil in human hearts. Therefore, we must take our stand against him.

We must stand our ground and stand firm against "the devil's schemes" (Eph. 6:11–14).

put on the full armor of God

We must not try to stand in our own strength, for God has provided a full array of armor to keep us safe when Satan and his demons attack us.

the belt of truth (eph. 6:14)
The Roman soldier's belt held every piece of armor in place. If truth characterizes us, the Father of Lies (John 8:44) will not be able to trip us up.

the breastplate of righteousness (eph. 6:14)
Just as a strong breastplate protected the Roman soldier's chest and heart, so righteousness protects our hearts. To have righteousness cover our hearts, we must belong to Christ, for we become the righteousness of God in him (2 Cor. 5:21). Righteous living, though, results from being sanctified by the Holy Spirit (3:17–18).

feet fitted with the gospel of peace (eph. 6:15)
A soldier needs sturdy footwear in order to stand firm in battle. So Ephesians 6:15 refers to having our "feet fitted with the readiness that comes from the gospel of peace." The sandals worn by Roman soldiers were heavy and studded with hobnails. They helped the soldiers stand firmly in place when an enemy attacked. Similarly, the gospel of peace is the firm foundation on which Christians stand. Satan would love to see us abandon the gospel, but we must always stand on its sure foundation.

the shield of faith (eph. 6:16)

The Roman soldier's shield was made of wood covered with linen and leather. It measured two-and-a-half feet wide and four feet long. It protected most of the soldier's body, especially when he crouched in a defensive position. An enemy often dipped his arrows in pitch and then set them ablaze before shooting them. The shield's cover would absorb and extinguish the fiery arrows upon impact. The imagery is clear. By taking the shield of faith, we render the Devil's fiery darts ineffective. The Evil One cannot defeat us if we resolutely trust in the Lord.

the helmet of salvation (eph. 6:17)

Roman soldiers protected their heads with metal helmets. The Devil and his demons try to attack our minds. They want to plant doubts, immoral notions, and discouraging thoughts in our minds. But they cannot succeed as long as we protect our minds with the helmet of salvation, which is our hope through Christ's work of sanctification in us (1 Thess. 5:8).

offensive weapons

Our struggle against the demonic is not entirely defensive. Two powerful offensive weapons are available to us.

the sword of the Spirit (eph. 6:17)

The sword of the Spirit is identified as "the word of God" (Eph. 6:17). The identification is appropriate because the Spirit inspired the Scriptures. The Bible is not merely human words, it is God's word. Just as a Roman soldier would not think of entering battle without his sword, we should not think of battling the forces of evil without a firm grip on the sword of the Spirit, the Word of God.

The way to fill our minds with thoughts that are from God and not from the Devil is to fill our minds with God's Word. We should be read the Bible every day and memorize passages. When the Devil came to tempt Jesus, how did Christ deal with him? By quoting Scripture. This is what we must do: fill our lives with God's Word, remove sinful thinking from our minds and replace it with godly thoughts.

Some key verses to memorize are as follows:

- Matthew 5—especially verses 1–16 (the Sermon on the Mount)
- Matthew 6:9–15—the Lord's Prayer
- Philippians 2—especially verses 5–11
- James 4:7—the need to submit to God and to resist the Devil

If we saturate our minds with Scripture, our lives will be fruitful (Ps. 1:1–3), and we will experience sanctification (John 17:17). All of this translates into victory over the Evil One.

prayer (eph. 6:18)

Prayer is the second offensive weapon available to us in our struggle against the Devil and his evil minions. Paul gave six instructions to guide our prayers. First, our prayers must be offered "in the Spirit" (Eph. 6:18). The Spirit prompts us to pray according to God's will. Romans 8:27 says, "The Spirit intercedes for God's people in accordance with the will of God."

Second, our prayers must be frequent. In other words, we should not pray only when trouble strikes us. We need to pray "on all occasions" (Eph. 6:18). Prayer should be a familiar activity in so-called good times as well as in bad times.

Third, we should offer "all kinds of prayers and request" (v. 18). We ought to examine our prayers to see whether they are full of repetitious phrases and therefore predictable. How urgent are our prayers? Are they most often "give me" prayers? Do we pray for God's glory or for personal benefit? Do we intercede for others? Do we confess our sins? Do we quote Scripture? Do we lift our hearts and voices in praise and thanksgiving when we pray?

Fourth, we need to be alert. A sleeping soldier is an easy target, and so is a believer who fails to stay alert. The apostle Peter also instructed us to be alert, because the Devil is ready to pounce on us (1 Pet. 5:8). We should recognize times when it is urgent to call on God for help. We should never face trials and temptations without praying. Nor should we fail to pray for fellow believers who are under satanic attack.

Fifth, we need to be persistent in prayer. A good soldier never gives up, never retreats. As good soldiers of the Lord, we must not stop praying. We need to be patient because help is on the way.

Finally, we need to pray for our fellow soldiers. In Ephesians 6:18, Paul requested prayer "for all the Lord's people." In verse 19, he requested prayer for himself. Although he was an apostle, he never outgrew the need for prayer. In our struggle with the Devil and his evil minions, we too will never outgrow the need to pray for one another and to have others pray for us. Intercessory prayer is vital to the holiness God desires to see in us. Satan trembles when he sees us on our knees.

conclusion

Our Enemy is diabolical, vicious, crafty, relentless, and powerful. He wants to draw us away from our holy heavenly Father and make us unholy. But we do not have to be victims. Our heavenly Father has made it possible for us to win the war against the Devil and his hordes of evil spirits. There will be many battles, but our Father has given us effective resources so we can emerge from each battle as victors not victims.

We can choose to use the resources or to try to go it alone. The war's outcome will be determined by how we choose. The wrong choice will result in personal unholiness, but the right choice will result in holiness that pleases God.

conclusion

We began *Unholiness* by recognizing Jesus Christ as the Savior of humanity. The incarnate Son of God is given the name Jesus by the angel Gabriel because he saves "his people from their sins" (Matt. 1:21). The apostle John declared, "The reason the Son of God appeared was to destroy the devil's work" (1 John 3:8). To redeem us, Christ must forgive us our sins and reconcile us to God. Thankfully, no sin is too great for Christ's atoning work on the cross and no reprobate so alienated from God to be beyond membership in the family of God.

Salvation, however, must be more than justification and adoption; there must be sanctification. If Christ truly is going to be our Savior, then he must set us free from bondage to sin and Satan. Our desires, our wills, and our actions must be transformed into Christlikeness. We must be cleansed of sin and empowered to triumph over the Devil and his minions. Thankfully, no power of sin or scheme of hell need have dominion over any Christian because of the Son's work in incarnation, life, death, resurrection, and exaltation.

the specific focus of *unholiness*

While this is a book on sanctification, more specifically it focuses on the forces that corrupt the image of God in humanity, make us slaves to sin and the Devil, and limit our growth in Christlikeness. Consequently, attention is given to one aspect of sanctification. However, most sound Christian teaching on sanctification has two major parts: one negative and the other positive. The negative identifies the problem that must be addressed if sanctification is to be possible: sin in its many expressions and all the Devil's work. The positive describes the goal or end of sanctification: holiness of heart and life, expressed in the love of God with our whole being, the love of neighbor as self, and obedience to God with an undivided will.

Unholiness intentionally concentrates on the negative, without completely ignoring the positive. Why? Because if holiness of heart and life is going to be experienced by us, then we need to know the problems and challenges we face. Before a disease can be treated effectively, it must be correctly diagnosed. Christians can't afford to be unaware of the forces that keep us from experiencing the end of our salvation. Ignorance here isn't just detrimental to our spiritual health; it's dangerous as well. Let's take a moment and review.

the forces that harm humanity

Rooted in the opening chapters of Genesis, the Christian doctrine of creation helps us see the beauty of human nature as embodied souls created by God. Our substance of body, soul, mind, and will is good. Through our formation as human beings, we bear the moral, natural, and political image of God. To be fully human, therefore, is to be like God, to walk in holy love. Because of our first parents' disobedience, however, our nature and personhood have been corrupted, individually and socially. We're subject to the lies and enticements of the Devil and the demonic. As we have discussed, we're slaves to the flesh, the world, and the Devil.

the flesh

The flesh is our most basic problem as human beings. The New Testament calls the corrupted divine image in us the flesh to express human nature and personhood under the reign of sin (Rom. 8:4–9; Gal. 5:17). Because of humanity's fall in the garden of Eden, the moral and natural image of God, expressed in our embodied nature as persons, has been left in devastation.

More specifically, the flesh represents the corrupted moral image of God in humanity, leaving us spiritually and morally bankrupt, helpless to change. Christianity has spoken about the moral image's degradation in two related ways: humanity's disordered love and its propensity to sin.

First, as made in God's moral image, we were formed as lovers. God intended humanity to share in the divine life existing between Father, Son, and Holy Spirit through loving God above all else and then loving neighbor as self. This love then properly ordered all other loves, desires, and relationships in creation. Now, because of the moral image's disrepair, we love ourselves and creation more than God, sending our desires and affections into chaos.

Second, the moral image made us holy in character. Following the righteous requirements of the law came easily to humanity. Our words, thoughts, and actions naturally aligned with God's will. Because of original sin, in contrast, we have a bent or propensity toward rebellion and disobedience. Internally, we balk at living the virtuous life, conforming to God's character, and doing what's right. Our fallen inclinations gravitate inevitably to sin.

In addition to the ruined moral image of God, the flesh includes the corrupted natural image, leaving humanity with impaired understanding, judgment, and will. As originally formed by God, the natural image enabled us to look at creation and all human relationships and to intuitively know its needs. After the fall, only vestiges of human rationality remain. We no longer see clearly the created order in which we live and how to act appropriately. Confusion reigns.

More distressingly, the corrupted natural image leaves us with a disabled will. In the garden, once we knew what needed to be said or done, we had the strength of will to do it. In the aftermath of our first parents' sin, the exercise of human will was crippled. Even when we see how we should live our lives, our will refuses to cooperate or is unable because of weakness. We can't follow through and do the good. Our will is incapable of aligning with God's law. We live under the tyranny of sin's strongholds because of the will's bondage to sin.

the world

The flesh isn't our only enemy. The New Testament names the world as another. While the flesh is identified with the corrupted moral and natural image of God in humanity, the world is related to the fallen political image.

First, the political image is what makes humanity a social creature, intimately connecting us to the created order and to other people. As God is not a solitary self, but a communion of divine persons inseparably united, the human individual mirrors the divine image through social relationships with other people. We image God in community as we live together under the lordship of Christ.

The world is the perversion of human community and institutions. It's society living covertly or openly in rebellion to the kingdom of God. Its origin is in humanity's corrupted political image. Through pervasive lies, distorted truths and actions, the world sets itself up as an alternate social order to the city of God, guided by values and ethics harmful to human relationships with God, each other, and creation.

The world as the city of man undermines our relationship with God by drawing our attention away from God and directing it to the physical world. It acts as if creation is all that exists. Materialism, hedonism, and atheism are expressions of its influence. The world also sabotages our human bonds by elevating the individual to the detriment of community or by lifting one group of people over another. Here, a person alone determines what is right and true for him- or herself, regardless of social consequences. Or one community asserts itself in prideful selfish rule over another. The world finally breaks our intimate connection to creation by blinding us to the physical world's inherent goodness and to our responsibility of wise stewardship. The world is manifested in our Gnostic attitudes toward creation and our unbridled consumption of it.

Second, the political image is what facilitates our formation as persons. As Father, Son, and Holy Spirit are constituted as distinct persons through their relationships and interactions with each other, we are as well. We develop who we are through a dynamic process combining our life experiences and relationships with our responses to them. Before the fall, we lived in perfect relationships of holy love with God, each other, and creation. Through active participation in these social relationships, mediated through the political image, our identity as beloved children in the family of God was forged.

The world is the corrupted expression of our socially constructed identities as God's daughters and sons, as followers of Jesus Christ, and as citizens of the city of God. The world works to make our age, families, economic classes, tribes, genders, ethnicities, and nationalities define of who we are.

For example, many Christians in the United States, whether they realize it or not, are formed by the world as young, white, Anglo-Saxon, middle class, American males and females to the neglect or loss of identity as Christian. Imperceptibly, one or more of these socially defining markers takes priority in forming their identity as persons. Instead of their citizenship in God's kingdom defining these other identifiers, their Christianity is subjugated to them.

The world also seeks to distort our identity through destructive and sinful social experiences. A man addicted to drugs is labeled an "addict"; a girl raped by a man is called a "victim"; a boy with learning problems is pigeonholed as "slow"; a woman without income and a home is branded "homeless"; a teenager who lies is identified as a "liar"; and someone who attempts to kill himself is "suicidal." The world actively takes our experiences of sin, shame, and evil and uses them to define who we are instead of identifying us as beloved children of God.

the Devil and demons

Unfortunately, our problems with the flesh and the world are compounded by the existence of Satan and demons. The forces that thwart our redemption in Christ are found not only in ourselves and in our social relationships, but also in creatures wholly different in nature than we are. Contrary to popular thought, and even to what many Christians believe today, there are real spiritual beings who seek to "steal and kill and destroy" us (John 10:10). While Satan is not omnipresent, omniscient, or omnipotent like God, he poses a ready threat to our salvation and a potent force for evil in the created order.

Like all beings made by God, Satan and his minions were created good and holy. Satan, who was originally named Lucifer, was an angel of light and given one of the most exalted positions in heaven at God's throne. He was overcome, however, with jealously and pride, eventually seeking to usurp God's rule with the help of other angels. For their sin, they were cast out of heaven, becoming the most malevolent beings in the created order. Because humanity is created in the image of God, their hatred turned toward humanity, leading our first parents' into sin and consequently us into ruin.

In the ongoing war they wage against humanity, the Devil and his evil forces primarily tempt us through the lust of the flesh, the lust of the eyes, and the pride of life. The Enemy uses natural human desires for food, comfort, companionship, sex, and human approval as occasions for temptation. He also employs the beauty bestowed by God in the created order to distract our attention from God and his divine will for our lives. Finally, the Devil and demons fan into flame false pride for our personal talents, accomplishments, and positions in life. They tempt us to believe that we are their ultimate source, not God.

The Devil's goal is to do real harm to us, physically and spiritually. He seeks to set himself up as our god and at times will perform counterfeit miracles to draw our worship. If he can't succeed in becoming our god, his assaults intensify. When we give our allegiance to Christ, Satan actively works to prevent us from establishing a strong and consistent prayer life, the key defensive and offensive weapon again the demonic. He conspires with the flesh and the world to keep believers defeated and discouraged. He wants to keep us slaves to sin. Our joy and peace in the Lord are targets for his schemes. Satan continually feeds us the lie that we are worthless to the cause of Christ or we have nothing to offer in service of God's kingdom, rendering us impotent as believers. He keeps us focused on our own vileness and sinfulness, rather than on our identity and resources as God's children.

sanctification as the remedy for the spiritual forces that harm humanity

Once we know what we're up against, we have a better idea of what Christ must do to save us. Sanctification is the remedy for the the flesh, the world, and the Devil. Through the Son of God's assumption of full human nature in the incarnation, through his life of human obedience to the will of God, through his victory over

Satan and every demonic scheme, through his atoning death on the cross, and through his bodily resurrection and exaltation to the right hand of God, sanctification is made possible. What Christ accomplished, the Holy Spirit applies to human lives. The Holy Spirit takes the full work of Christ and imparts it to us.

Christ redeems us from the flesh through the Spirit's reestablishment of the moral image of God in us and the ongoing restoration of the natural. First, he transforms our desires, so that we begin to earnestly desire God and the reign of God in our lives. He then empowers our will, breaking the power of sin, enabling us to walk in obedience to what we know of God. Finally, he removes our bent and propensity toward rebellion, disobedience, and selfishness, replacing it with an undivided love of God and neighbor. He makes holy love and obedience to God the natural response of our lives.

Because our reasoning, understanding, and judgment can't be fully restored in this life, we continue to be subject to mistakes, misunderstandings, and clouded judgment. However, we can grow in these areas as we learn more about God and his Word, healthy human relationships, and ourselves.

Christ redeems us from the world by the Spirit's continuing renewal of the political image of God in us through the church. In this earthly city of God, we experience the community for which we've been created as far as possible in fallen creation and learn to walk in victory over the world. Here, we learn to discern the distorted messages and lies given by the world, and we are formed as Christians, an identity that sanctifies all other markers given to us through personal experience and by larger society.

Christ redeems us from the Devil by delivering us from Satan's clutches in salvation and equipping us with both defensive and offensive arms to thwart his schemes. When we become Christians, Satan's claim on our lives is revoked and our servitude to him broken. The Spirit then gives us the full armor of God to withstand his attacks: the belt of truth, the breastplate of righteousness, feet fitted with the gospel of peace, the shield of faith, and the helmet of salvation (Eph. 6:14–17). We are also furnished with weapons so we can take the war to the Enemy: the sword of the Spirit and prayer (vv. 17–18). Walking in victory over the Devil is our birthright as Christians.

the image of sanctification in early rituals of baptism

Perhaps no greater imagery of our sanctification exists in the church than the early rituals connected to baptism in Christianity's first five centuries. First was the rite of exorcism. Before candidates were baptized, they appeared before a group of Christian leaders who had the gift of spiritual discernment. After extensive examination, any demonic presence was identified and exorcised from them. Then, each person would vocally renounce Satan and all spiritual forces of wickedness, followed by a confession of personal faith in the triune God.

Next was the rite of water baptism. Here candidates descended individually into water and were baptized by an elder or deacon in the name of the Father, Son, and Holy Spirit, the name in whom they had just confessed faith. Water baptism signified cleansing from sin, emergence from gestational waters into spiritual birth, a descent of death to sin, and an ascent of resurrection to a holy life.

The rite of chrismation followed. Newly baptized Christians were immediately anointed with oil and prayed over with the laying on of hands, pointing to the empowering work of the Holy Spirit in their lives. Their ears were anointed so they would be ready to hear the word of God; then the thumb on their right hand, empowering their lives to become instruments of righteousness; then the big toe on the right foot so they would be enabled to walk in the way of holiness. The remaining oil was poured over their head so their whole lives would then be consecrated to God.

Finally, these rites culminated in the eucharistic celebration. Straightway after chrismation, believers participated for the first time in Holy Communion with all other baptized Christians. They joined their new family at Christ's table to eat the meal he prepared: his broken body and shed blood. The immediacy of their Communion experience pointed to the ultimate end of their salvation: to be called out of the world and joined to a new community—the church, the family of God, the city of God; and to enjoy a new identity in this community—Christians, the sons and daughters of God, citizens of Zion.

Each aspect of these rites points to the sanctifying work of God in our lives: liberation from bondage to Satan and his minions, cleansing from sin and a new life of holiness in Christ, restoration of the ability to hear God's word and to learn his ways, empowerment to serve and walk in holiness, wholehearted devotion to God, and a new identity (radically different from the one given to us by the world) through inclusion in a new human community—the church.

steps you can take to address harmful spiritual forces

The early church believed these rituals point to the normative Christian life. Together, they paint a picture of what every Christian should experience: freedom from the flesh, the world, and the Devil. Unfortunately, for a multitude of reasons, many believers settle for a life in Christ that has little resemblance to what we have described. Is this you? If so, here are some concrete actions you can take to realize more fully Christ's sanctifying grace in your life.

identify the specific spiritual forces that oppress and defeat you

The premise of *Unholiness* is that we must know what forces are aligned against our souls. Therefore, begin by examining your life with the help of the Holy Spirit. Ask the Spirit to help identify areas of occasional and ongoing struggle in your life. If you have trusted Christian friends who know you well, ask for their honest assessment of your life.

First, do you struggle with aspects of the flesh? What is the state of your heart, will, and actions? While not exhaustive, more specific questions like the following can be helpful: Do you truly desire God and the kingdom of God more than anything else? Are you intentionally disobeying God? Do you have the power to walk in outward obedience to the known will of God? Are there any strongholds of sin in your life over which you have little or no control? Does the love of God and neighbor come naturally to you, even in difficult circumstances? Does the fruit of the Spirit so define your life that you walk in inward conformity to God's known will?

Second, are you compromised in any way by the world? In what ways are you being formed by the city of man? While not a complete list, here are some possible questions useful for exploration: What are the values and ethics that direct decisions in your personal and family life? As you look at what's happening in human society and the world, how do you respond? Do you regularly practice self-denial or are you driven by the need for immediate self-gratification? Do family ties, ethnic identity, national citizenship, economic class, sexual gender, or sexual identity define your Christianity or does your Christianity define them? And have you allowed any particular sin, shame, or experience of evil to label you more than being a beloved child of God?

Finally, are you susceptible to the schemes of the Devil and his forces? Do you fall prey to his devices? Some beneficial questions for reflection include: Do you struggle persistently with real doubt about the existence of a loving and just God? Do you continually question God's love for you? Do thoughts of self-harm or suicide cross your mind? Are you frequently distracted from reading the Scriptures, personal prayer, and committed participation in a local church? And do you persistently dwell on your failures and inadequacies as a Christian?

go to Jesus Christ in full surrender

If you want to experience freedom from the forces that oppress your soul, you must surrender your life fully to Jesus Christ. You can't hold back any part of your life from God. You need to give it all to him—your dreams, talents, fears, emotional wounds, money, strongholds of sin, divided heart, and pride. Withhold nothing. Consecrate all areas of your life to Christ—areas over which you have control, as well as those over which you have no control. Christ must have it all.

If you are unwilling or unable to do so, Christ's sanctifying work through the Spirit is seriously compromised. If this is you, ask Jesus to change your desires and then ask him for the power to fully surrender your life to him. The real work of sanctification begins here.

believe that Christ through the Holy Spirit can sanctify you

Once surrendered, believe that Jesus Christ through the power of the Holy Spirit can bring freedom from the forces you've identified through personal examination. By God's grace through faith, you can be gradually redeemed from some of these over time, while others in definite moments.

Certain forces are overcome through progressive sanctification. They are treated by Christ through (1) growth in knowledge, wisdom, and understanding of God's will for our lives; (2) the formation of our identity as the beloved children of God, as citizens of the city of God; and (3) our increased familiarity with Satan's schemes. All of which bring greater conformity to Christlikeness steadily into our lives.

Other forces are dealt with in decisive moments of divine grace. In our Wesleyan tradition, we associate these with conversion and entire sanctification, but they need not be limited to them. These forces of sin and Satan are broken by Christ through the Spirit-filled life, setting us free from the power of sin and Satan's hold which enables us to walk in outward obedience to God's revealed will, and orienting us in the love of God and neighbor so that the fruit of the Spirit becomes the natural propensity of our lives which brings inward conformity.

Both progressive and entire sanctification are difficult to believe, although the latter far more than the former. Some of your forces may only be addressed through progressive sanctification, while others in definable moments of sanctification, such as entire sancti-fication. If you desire the sanctified life, you must believe that Christ can do both. If you lack faith, ask the Lord to give you faith.

seek God's sanctifying grace in the church

Through progressive and entire sanctification, the image of God in humanity is restored and we become more fully human. However, in the end, the full restoration of the *imago dei* happens in the church. Such renewal of the moral, natural, and political image of God in us doesn't come by dabbling in the church, but by full par-ticipation in the church. The church is necessary because it is the primary means of God's saving, sustaining, and sanctifying grace in the world. Furthermore, only in the church can we, as the city of God, navigate the treacherous waters of the world. In this earthly city of God, we experience the community for which we've been created as far as possible in fallen creation and learn to walk in vic-tory over the world. Therefore, if you are going to overcome the forces that oppress you, whatever they are, you need to commit and be active in a local church where the historic marks are manifested: the preaching of the pure Word of God, the due administration of the sacraments, and the community rightly ordered.

notes

Introduction
1. C. S. Lewis, *The Great Divorce* (New York: Macmillan, 1946), 72.
2. Ibid., 65–68.

Chapter 1
1. John Hospers, *An Introduction to Philosophical Analysis*, 3rd ed. (Oxford: Routledge, 1990), 310.
2. David Hume, *Hume: Dialogues Concerning Natural Religion and Other Writings*, ed. Dorothy Coleman, Cambridge Texts in the History of Philosophy (Cambridge, UK: Cambridge University Press, 2007), 68–89.
3. John Wesley, "The New Birth," Sermon 45, *Sermons II*, ed. Albert C. Outler, vol. 2 of The Bicentennial Edition of the Works of John Wesley (Nashville: Abingdon Press, 1985), § I.1.

Chapter 2

1. John Chrysostom, *Homilies on Genesis 1–17*, trans. Robert C. Hill, Fathers of the Church, vol. 74 (Washington, DC: The Catholic University of America Press, 1986), 207–222.
2. Augustine, *Confessions*, trans. Henry Chadwick, Oxford World Classics (Oxford: Oxford University Press, 2009), book 8, section 9.

Chapter 3

1. See the "Westminster Larger Catechism" in Valarie R. Hotchkiss and Jaroslav Pelikan, *Creeds and Confessions of Faith in the Christian Tradition*, vol. II (London: Yale University Press), 619–620.
2. George Dokos, *A Manual of Confessions by Our Righteous God-Bearing Father Nikodemos the Hagiorite* (Thessalonica: Uncut Mountain Press, 2006), 83.
3. C. S. Lewis, *The Screwtape Letters* (San Francisco, Harper Collins, 1941), 3.

Chapter 4

1. Augustine, *Confessions*, book 1, section 1.
2. This quote is a popular revision of what Blaise Pascal stated in his philosophical work *Pensées*, trans. A. J. Krailsheimer, Penguin Classics (London: Penguin Books, 1995), 148.
3. Augustine, *The City of God*, trans. Henry Bettenson (London: Penguin Books, 2003), 53–737.
4. Thomas C. Oden, quoted by Rich Nathan in *Who Is My Enemy? Welcoming People the Church Rejects* (Grand Rapids, MI: Zondervan, 2002), 50.

Chapter 5

1. H. Richard Niebuhr, *Christ and Culture* (New York: Harper and Row, 1951).
2. Ibid., 80–81.
3. Ibid., 171–207.
4. John G. Stackhouse Jr., "In the World, but . . ." in *Christianity Today* 46, no. 5 (April 22, 2002): 80.

5. Letter to Mandell Creighton, published in John Emerich Edward Dalberg-Acton, *Historical Essays and Studies*, eds. John Neville Figgis and Reginald Vere Laurence (London: Macmillan, 1907).

Chapter 6
1. John White, *The Fight* (Downers Grove, IL: InterVarsity, 1976), 81.

Chapter 7
1. C. S. Lewis, *The Screwtape Letters* (New York: Harper Collins, 1961), ix.

2. W. E. Vine, *An Expository Dictionary of New Testament Words* (London: Oliphants, 1953), 278.

3. ElRay L. Christiansen, "Q&A: Questions and Answers," *New Era* (July 1975): 49, accessed May 22, 2015, https://www.lds.org/newera/1975/07/qa-questions-and-answers?lang=eng.

4. Wilbur O'Donovan, *Biblical Christianity in African Perspective*, 2nd ed. (Buckinghamshire, England: Paternoster Press, 1997), 196.

5. Charles Spurgeon, *The Devotional Classics of C. H. Spurgeon: Morning & Evening I & II*, vol. 1 (Mulberry, IN: Sovereign Grace Publishers, 2008), August 7.

6. John Wesley, "Sermon XLII, Satan's Devices," in *The Works of John Wesley*, 3rd ed. (Kansas City, MO: Beacon Hill, 1979), 33–34.